SMOLLETT STUDIES

BY

CLAUDE E. JONES

UNIVERSITY OF CALIFORNIA PUBLICATIONS IN ENGLISH

Volume 9, No. 2, pp. xii + 29–134

SMOLLETT STUDIES

BY

CLAUDE E. JONES

Phaeton Press

New York

1970

Originally Published 1942
Reprinted 1970

PR
3696
J6
1970

Published by PHAETON PRESS, INC.
Library of Congress Catalog Card Number - 70-128188
SBN 87753-048-3

To the Smollettians:

JOHN MOORE

ROBERT ANDERSON

SIR WALTER SCOTT

CHARLES DICKENS

ERNEST HENLEY

THOMAS SECCOMBE

EDWARD S. NOYES

HOWARD SWAZEY BUCK

LEWIS M. KNAPP

LOUELLA NORWOOD

EUGÈNE JOLIAT

GEORGE M. KAHRL

This slight token is inscribed

PREFACE

Tobias Smollett, one of the most versatile and prolific of English eighteenth-century men of letters, was, in turn, naval surgeon, physician, novelist, poet, editor, playwright, party writer, historian, translator, satirist, critic, traveler, and literary nabob among the Grub Street hack writers. His activities included supervision of translations of Le Sage, Voltaire, and Cervantes; editorial work for the second great English review and for the *British Magazine,* which contained the first serialized novel (his own *Launcelot Greaves*); at least two original contributions to medical literature, as well as editorial work on the century's most important obstetrical treatise; authorship of one of the most widely discussed travel books of the time, and editorship of another; and the production of four novels, including two which have attained to the dignity of "classics." One of the most important men of a period which included such figures as Johnson, Goldsmith, Boswell, Sheridan, Hume, Adam Smith, Fielding, and Richardson—most of whom were his friends,—Smollett represents the professional littérateur of a diversitarian age.

In this study I am primarily concerned with Smollett as critic of the navy and as writer for the *Critical Review.* These two aspects of his experience have elicited particular notice from Smollett enthusiasts—among whom Scott and Henley are not the least,—but no extensive treatment of either phase has yet appeared. He seems to have made enthusiastic friends and bitter enemies, the latter as a result of his politico-journalistic and critical work, so that contemporary accounts of his abilities vary considerably. Smollett, like many of those who engage in literary warfare, can only now, a hundred and fifty years after his death, begin to receive his due; yet even today apologists for the men who were his enemies are prone to spatter their eulogies with contempt for "Toby."

I am primarily concerned, first, with the novelist's experience in the British navy and his use of material concerning the service; and, second, with his work as a literary critic. The following study is not exhaustive, because there are still many lacunae in our knowledge of Smollett's life and activities, gaps which, it is hoped, will eventually be filled, by Professor Lewis M. Knapp, whose patient researches have done much to enlighten us already, and by others interested in the novelist. Dr. Knapp's projected life of Smollett is, however, a work *de longue haleine,* and I feel that already enough material is available for a general picture of Smollett as editor of the *Critical Review* and as a writer whose knowledge of the navy resulted in frequent and illuminating treatment of the service at its worst.

As explanation of Smollett's bitterness concerning the navy, a general factual introduction is necessary. Some account of his experience and versatility as a man of letters must also precede the treatment of his career as editor of the *Critical.* As for the appendixes, the first is Smollett's attack on Admiral Knowles. The second relates directly to Smollett and the *Critical Review;* it comprises a list of attacks on the *Critical,* 1756–1771 (Appendix B1), and the *Visitor's* satirical letter of March, 1756, which is extremely rare (Appendix B2). The third and fourth appendixes present two obscure and generally unavailable literary pieces which have been ascribed to Smollett; the fifth and last consists of two letters to him from Dr. John Gray, historian and poet, who became one of the novelist's best friends.

I hope that the errors, from which no such work as this can be completely free, will be rather of omission than commission. Year by year new material illuminating the life and work of Tobias Smollett is uncovered, and some day the marked set of the *Critical* may appear—but until that time we must proceed slowly and by devious ways. With the fragments that appear in letters, diaries, contracts, attacks, and eulogies we must break through the veil of anonymity that conceals the identity of the authors of unsigned articles in this second of great English monthly reviews. Such a method can never accomplish perfection, and new manuscripts and hitherto unexamined publications will doubtless shed more light on various individuals concerned with the *Review* or with Smollett in the navy. I only hope that I have made the most of the material which was accessible to me.

CLAUDE E. JONES

West Los Angeles, California.

ACKNOWLEDGMENTS

THE FIRST of these studies, "Smollett and the Navy," was begun in 1933 under the aegis of Professor Horace A. Eaton, biographer of De Quincey, at Syracuse University, Syracuse, New York. During its development, I was able to work for some time at the public libraries of New York City and Philadelphia, as well as in the Library of Congress.

The second, "Smollett and the *Critical Review,*" is one of the results of an extensive study of that periodical, undertaken at Johns Hopkins University under the guidance of Professors Raymond D. Havens and Hazleton Spencer. While I was working at Johns Hopkins, and later in California, the following libraries gave me information, either by correspondence or by affording me reading facilities: the Library of Congress; the Huntington; the Folger Shakespeare; Columbia University; Yale University; the University of Pennsylvania; the public libraries of New York City, Philadelphia, Boston, and Baltimore; the Peabody Institute; the Library Company of Philadelphia; the British Museum; and the University of California, both at Berkeley and at Los Angeles. To those staff members who have assisted in the present work I offer sincere thanks.

To the following individuals much is owing, debts which will indeed be hard to repay: the late Colonel Fielding H. Garrison; Professor Horace A. Eaton, of Syracuse University; Professor Edward S. Noyes, of Yale University; Professor Lewis M. Knapp, of Colorado College; Professors Raymond D. Havens, Kemp Malone, and Hazleton Spencer, all of Johns Hopkins University; Dr. John C. French, Librarian, and Mr. Louis M. Kuethe, Assistant Librarian, both of Johns Hopkins; Professors Alfred E. Longueil and Edward Niles Hooker, of the University of California, Los Angeles; the Misses Kazuko Suzuki and Elizabeth C. McCoy, and Mrs. Claude E. Jones, all of Los Angeles. I wish also to express most sincere appreciation of the many kindnesses and the encouragement which I have received from Professor Gustave O. Arlt, of the University of California, Los Angeles.

C. E. J.

CONTENTS

SMOLLETT AND THE NAVY

I. SMOLLETT AND THE NAVY

THE BRITISH NAVY IN 1740

WHEN the "War of Jenkyns' Ear" was declared with Spain in 1739, the British navy consisted of one hundred and four ships of the line.[1] These were divided according to the number of guns carried into rates, or classes, as follows: first rates of one hundred guns; second, of from eighty-four to ninety; third, from sixty-four to eighty; and fourth, from fifty to sixty.[2] Genuine frigates, mounting twenty-eight guns, were not built until about 1748; but they were to become the backbone of the navy by the time of Nelson. The "great ships," all those with over eighty guns, remained at dock during the winter, while the others kept the sea for twelve months a year. There were, of course, such smaller vessels as bombs, ketches, and supply ships; but the brunt of the fighting fell on the first four rates.

The English man-of-war in 1740 was three-masted, square-rigged, and carried a spanker. It was some hundred and fifty feet long and fifty wide. The great ships had three decks; fourth rates had two. Sixty-gun ships carried four hundred men, and third rates had a complement of six hundred, which gives some idea of the crowded conditions prevailing.

The naval force of England was divided into three fleets, each having its own admiral and his two junior flag officers. In time of war another officer, an "admiral of Great Britain," was added. Promotion to a flag was based primarily on service, a practice which resulted in superannuated leaders. Later, in 1741, retirement was made possible, and consequently promotion came to younger, more active, men.

Each ship had to carry men to fight her and repair her, men to set the course and men to steer it, surgeons to tend the sick

---

[1] Cf. [Anon.], *A Compleat History of the Present War with Spain* (London, 1742), p. 18.
[2] Cf. William Clowes [and others], *The Royal Navy*, III (Boston, 1899), 7.

and cooks to feed the healthy; she was a microcosm complete in almost every detail. Those who manned the ships were, on the whole, brutal and coarse. The captain, emperor of this little world, was responsible for everything that happened aboard. He held court-martial and, in 1740, had full powers of life and death when at sea. Under him served a corps of experts, and the lieutenants carried out his orders on watch. The specialists included such officers as the master, who was navigating officer, the surgeon and his mates, the chaplain, purser, and steward. The petty or warrant officers were the sailmakers, carpenters, boatswains, and gunners, and their mates.

Surgeons, most of whom came from among the licentiates of Edinburgh, were commissioned after examination at Surgeon's Hall in London. Chaplains were appointed by the government, just as the ministers ashore were presented with "livings." Commissioned officers, however, might enter the service in several ways,[3] and were supposed to rise through promotion. There were three ways in which a future lieutenant might begin his career: by appointment, with a letter from the king; by admission from a training school; or by promotion from "before the mast." The first two groups were composed of gentlemen, the third, of servicemen. The youngest gentlemen were called "midshipmen"; the servicemen were nicknamed "tarpawlins."

Sailors either volunteered or were impressed. Even during times of peace it was practically impossible to man properly the necessary ships. In 1739, Walpole was faced with the problem of carrying on war with one-third of his ships idle because they lacked crews.[4] The admiralty laid an embargo on all coastwise ships in an effort to obtain men. Justices of the peace sent criminals to Portsmouth, and the "Lord Mayor's men," notorious rakehells

---

[3] See David Hannay's "Navy and Navies," *Ency. Brit.,* 11th ed.

[4] That Walpole appreciated the seriousness of this condition is evident from his remark to Sir Charles Norriss, "I must ... again add, what has been the burden of my song in every council these four months—Oh! seamen, seamen, seamen!" Quoted by Lord John Hervey in *Memoirs of the Reign of George the Second* (London, 1884), III, 368.

and insolvent debtors, came down from London. The bounty for volunteers was increased from forty-two to one hundred shillings for an able-bodied seaman.[5] Even so, it was impossible to obtain enough men, and when Anson sailed for the South Seas on September 14, 1740, he was forced to take on board over two hundred pensioners from Greenwich Hospital, some of whom were septuagenarians.[6]

Press gangs combed every waterfront town, seizing any able-bodied man they met. Fletcher says, "Almost any man of the middle class might be seized in the public street by a band of armed men, beaten, pinioned, and shipped off to serve the king whether he would or no."[7] Men returning from long voyages were liable to be pressed from their ships and, with no time ashore, sent back to sea in a service that might hold them virtual prisoners for years. Many plans were suggested for doing away with this method, which was continually in force from the time of Elizabeth to late in the nineteenth century—as late as 1858 eight hundred men were pressed in one year from London alone.[8] The effects of impressment on personnel may be imagined. To insure against desertion, which was common despite the death penalty, the officers kept their crews confined aboard ship at all times possible.

The men thus brought into the service were first sent to a guard ship, where they were deloused and kept until allotted to one of the regular ships. The sanitary conditions aboard these guard ships were horrible. Dr. Richard Lind says of the guard ship at The Nore,

... experience has shown how fatal she has proved to the health and lives of many seamen; and that this ship has become a seminary of contagion to the whole fleet. One diseased person from the street, or clothes from a prison, have often conveyed infection aboard, which

---

[5] Clowes, *op. cit.*, III, 18.
[6] *Ibid.*, III, 20.
[7] "The Press Gang," *Nineteenth Century*, L (Nov., 1901), 771.
[8] *Ibid.*, p. 765.

it has been extremely difficult afterwards to get quit of. For the confined and corrupted air in a large crowded ship, greatly favours the spreading of this contagion, and the exertion of its utmost malignity. From this source, the environs of Portsmouth and Plymouth have more than once been annoyed with an almost pestilential contagion, which certain regulations might, in all probability, have effectually prevented.[9]

He states, further, "I have known 1,000 men continued together in a guardship, some hundred of whom had neither a bed nor so much as a change of linen. I have seen many of them brought into hospital in the same clothes and shirts they had on when pressed several months before."[10]

Once aboard ship, raw material of the type obtained by such recruiting methods had literally to be knocked into shape by brutal methods and kept in hand by vicious punishments. It was well said at the time that "anyone who would go to sea for pleasure, would go to hell for a pastime."[11] The usual punishment was flogging, which, like pressing, was a heritage from the days of Elizabeth. For minor offenses it was administered aboard ship, at the head of the gangway.

Aboard the *Chichester,* on which Smollett served during the Cartagena campaign, there were at least two such punishments, both of which he probably witnessed, inasmuch as he would have been among the general muster which was called on such occasions. On December 18, 1740, "Samuel Murray was whipt for mutiny because the steward would not give him his meat raw & for beating the cooper."[12] Just three months later, "John Attoway

[9] In *An Essay on the Most Effectual Means of Preserving the Health of Seamen* (London, 1757), p. 12.

[10] *Ibid.,* p. 15.

[11] Quoted by W. J. Aylward in "The Old Man-of-War's Man," *Scribner's,* XL (Jan., 1914), 38.

[12] From a journal kept by Lieutenant Robert Watkins, of the *Chichester,* as quoted by Lewis Knapp in his article, "Naval Scenes in 'Roderick Random,'" *PMLA,* XLIX (June, 1934), 594. Mr. Knapp's researches in the Public Record Office supplement an article by W. G. Perrin in *The Mariner's Mirror, The Journal of the Society for Nautical Research,* X (Jan., 1924), 94, where for the first time Smollett was accurately placed aboard H.M.S. *Chichester,* and a summary of the entries in the ship's log relating to the surgeon's second mate was made available.

Run the Gauntlett 3 Times thro the Ships Company for Theft and James Gunnehorn was whipt at the Gangway."[13] The following is a good picture of how this was done:

... the boatswain's shrill pipe and call of "All ha-a-ands witness punishment, ahoy!" summons the crew to the waist and gangway. Then, when the officers, in full uniform, are grouped on the quarterdeck, and the marines are drawn up on the poop with fixed bayonets, and the quartermasters have rigged the grating against the bulwark, and the boatswain and his mates are ready with their canvas bags containing the cruel *cats*—then the Master-at-arms, with rattan in hand, aided by a marine, brings forward the poor prisoner, and assists him to strip, at the word of command, for punishment. When the cat descends wielded by the brawny arm of the boatswain's mate, the Master-at-arms, in a loud voice, counts "one," "two," and so on up to a dozen; and he holds a cup of water ready to apply to the lips of the sufferer, if the latter should appear likely to faint.[14]

More serious crimes led to "whipping through the fleet," of which the colorful description in Nordhoff and Hall's *Mutiny on the Bounty*[15] is probably the best to be found. This punishment consisted of a small-boat tour by the criminal and the men who flogged him to all the ships stationed at the harbor where the punishment took place. Aboard each ship sailors and marines were drawn up to witness punishment; at every gangway the boat stopped, the sentence was read aloud, and the specified number of lashes administered. It is significant that, in 1799, Admiral Sir Hyde Parker issued instructions for a surgeon to be present "to see that no greater punishment is inflicted than the men can safely bear."[16] This humane provision, made as it was at the very end of the century, however, did not obtain during the 1740's, when the victim usually died before the sentence was completely carried out.

---

[13] *Ibid.*

[14] [Anon.], "Our Man-o'-War's Men," *Dublin Univ. Mag.*, XLVI (Dec., 1855), 657. This was written after the punishment had been reduced to a maximum of twelve lashes, a restriction not in effect during the first half of the eighteenth century.

[15] New York, 1932, pp. 22–25.

[16] His original order book (Aug., 1799, to July, 1800) from which this quotation is taken, I examined in manuscript at the New York Public Library.

Opinions as to the efficacy of flogging varied considerably, as evaluations of the social value of capital punishment do today. The more hardened seamen often took ordinary sentences stoically, even defiantly, as a matter of pride. As late as 1826, an anonymous reviewer in *Blackwood's* says that "flogging is a privilege of our seamen," and adds, "But what exaggerating and dishonest idiots are they who confound the disgraceful agonies of tortured nature with a little smarting between the shoulders, and down even to the rump."[17] More sensitive observers were revolted by this practice, however, as well as doubtful of its value. By our own standards, two centuries later, it seems indefensible.

The maximum punishments were shooting and hanging. Shooting was usually reserved for officers (like Admiral Byng, who was executed on board the *Monarque*); hanging was much more common. Mutineers, pirates, and deserters were all rewarded with a slipknot. As this was the customary penalty ashore for petty larceny, as well as for murder, it is not surprising that such a service as the navy should have resorted to it frequently. When men are as completely under the power of their officers as were the seamen of this period, the types of punishment are only limited by the imaginations of those who inflict them. Further, the severity with which they are carried out depends on the physical endurance of the man punished and the commanding officer's need for him.

The eighteenth-century navy, then, was marked by wholesale impressment, the general practice of flogging, and unbelievably poor sanitary conditions.[18] Something has already been said of hygiene aboard the guard ships. That prevailing on the men-of-war was little better, and Smollett's picture of the sick bay of the *Thunder* is substantially true. The absence of personal cleanliness

---

[17] XIX (March, 1826), 372.

[18] These also provided part of Melville's theme in *White-Jacket,* published a century after *Roderick Random,* and, much more than its predecessor, intended as propaganda for naval reform. Charles Roberts Anderson has recently published an excellent study of this phase of Melville's work: *Melville in the South Seas* (New York, 1939).

was inevitable where men received no uniforms but were forced to wear the clothes in which they entered the service until these hung about them in rags. Further, it was impossible to wash oneself, and men with contagious diseases, fearing the surgeon's knife or purge, mingled freely with the rest of the crew.

In port the men suffered from jail fever or malaria, depending on the climate. On long sea voyages scurvy took a high toll although honest efforts were made to fight it.[19] That Smollett himself spent some time in the sick bay as patient is indicated by the fact that among the deductions from his pay recorded in the ship's musters appears the item, "Hospital 10/8."[20] We hear little of venereal disease although it was rampant in all classes of society. Probably it was so common as to provoke no comment; besides, even the inefficacious treatments of the time were too expensive for a sailor. In fact, as late as the middle of the nineteenth century, navy men suffering from syphilis or gonorrhea had to pay the ship's surgeon for individual treatments or go without them.

With these conditions in mind, the reader finds an interesting contrast between the status of a merchant seaman and that of a naval seaman as described by a *Critical* reviewer, possibly Smollett himself, in 1759:

A sailor in the merchant service lives free and without controul; eats as much as he can swallow; fears no court-martial, or personal outrage; can stay on board or go ashore as he thinks proper; is exposed to no danger but that which is inseparably connected with a seafaring life; gratifies his roving disposition, by drifting from place to place; enjoys much greater wages than those that are given in the king's service; has some opportunities of trade; and if he either dislikes his ship, his commander, his messmates, his voyage, he seeks another commander without hesitation or restraint. On the other hand, a sailor on

---

[19] Cf. John Pringle, "A Discourse upon Some Late Improvements for Preserving the Health of Mariners," in James Cook, *A Voyage towards the South Pole, and Round the World* (London, 1777), II, 369–396.

[20] Quoted by Knapp in article cited, *PMLA*, XLIX (June, 1934), 594. Smollett's own illness may have been, as Knapp suggests here, the original for Random's experience in chapter 34 of the novel.

board of a king's ship is restricted to an allowance of provision, and
that not always of the best species; he is subject to controul and personal outrage, under a succession of officers, from the captain to the
boatswain's driver; he is exposed to flagellation, stripes, shackles, court-
martials, death and maiming from the enemy. His wages are small
and ill paid; he has no opportunity to turn his money to advantage;
he is liable to be dragged unwillingly to long voyages, tedious stations,
and unhealthy climates; he is debarred all intercourse with his friends
on shore, guarded and watched on board as a prisoner of war; and
if he should escape, and be retaken, is in danger of being shot for a
deserter. Such are the most obvious particulars in which the two services differ; and who, in his right wits, would prefer the former to the
latter situation?"[21]

Graft and other forms of corruption for which opportunities
were scant in the merchant marine flourished in the navy; every-
one, from the admiralty commissioners to the marines on guard
at the navy yards, gave and accepted bribes. This custom was so
deeply entrenched at the time that it prevailed not only in the
service but throughout the whole structure of government as
well. Even men as honest as Nelson and Anson found it impossible to effect any lasting reforms in this direction. In a navy
where personal connections were more valuable than courage
and ability, where politics was more important than the service
itself,[22] and where officers preferred a rival's disgrace to victory,
little could be accomplished.

The whole government was inefficient, and nowhere was this
more apparent than in the navy, particularly in regard to stores.
The poorness of ship's fare was notorious; in fact, at no time
during the first three centuries of the service's existence was the
food good or, indeed, even consistently decent. In 1740, when
Anson was outfitting for his voyage, innumerable delays were

---

[21] *Critical Review,* VIII (Sept., 1759), 206–207. The book reviewed here is Harvay's
Reason for Augmentation.

[22] While Admiral Vernon was on the expedition to Cartagena, his friends in England
secured his election to Parliament; and Admiral Byng was a member of the House of
Lords when he was tried. Cf. *Original Letters to an Honest Sailor* [i.e., Admiral Vernon]
(London, 1746), p. 36.

caused by the leisurely fashion in which his superiors acted, until, ready to sail, he found that forty-two out of the *Gloucester's* seventy-two puncheons of beef were "stinking."[23] In December of the same year, 1740, Lieutenant Watkins of Smollett's ship, the *Chichester,* notes: "Had a Survey and condemned Eighteen Hundred and Ninety five pounds of Cheese."[24]

With the exceptions of such "iron rations" as salt meat, biscuit, cheese, and beer, the food for an expedition was carried by private contractors in sloops which accompanied the fleet. Often these boats were lost at sea; at best they served to slacken considerably the progress of the warships. The food aboard a ship of the line was neither attractive nor wholesome. Roots, such as potatoes and turnips, were practically unknown at the time. Biscuit and salt beef were the staples, eked out with soggy puddings and dried fish, and washed down with small beer. Vernon introduced grog, or spirits mixed with water; later the water was omitted. The officers, who messed separately, fared considerably better because they brought with them wine and other delicacies. For the seamen, however, Monday, Wednesday, and Friday were "banyan days," when no meat was served. On tropical service, when fresh fruits could be obtained, such fasts were a blessing, but elsewhere they resulted in much hardship.

This, then, was the British navy of 1740; yet its personnel, drawn from the dregs of society by press gang and jail delivery, laid the foundation of that mastery of the sea which became an actuality at Trafalgar with the command, "Engage the enemy more closely." Rotten hulks sailed by ill-fed jailbirds under the command of incompetent and brutal officers characterized the service. And if *Roderick Random* was not designed, like Melville's *White-Jacket* a century later, to remedy conditions known by the author to be intolerable to crew and decent officers alike,

---

[23] Cf. John Masefield's introduction to Richard Walter's *A Voyage Round the World . . . by George Anson* (New York, 1930), p, xv.

[24] Quoted by Knapp in article cited, *PMLA,* XLIX (June, 1934), 596.

nevertheless Smollett's critics have not hesitated to credit him with some part in the movement which culminated in the sweeping reforms effected by Admiral Lord Nelson at the end of the century. Certainly *Random* was extremely popular, edition following close on edition for a century and a half after its first publication, and the effectiveness of its denunciation of the navy must have grown as the English came to feel that all Englishmen, even sailors, deserved justice and decency.

SMOLLETT AND THE NAVY

Every critic who considers the novels and plays of Tobias Smollett remarks upon the *vraisemblance* of his description of the British navy and its personnel. With the exception of Mr. David Hannay's comments,[1] however, little analysis has been made of the naval aspects of his work. The purpose of this section is to evaluate Smollett's treatment of the navy of his time by comparing his description with other sources and with the evidence of modern historical research.

Roderick Random's acquaintance with realistic navy characters and their code begins when he meets "Beau" Jackson. It is true that Random's uncle, Lieutenant Bowling, has appeared before this time, but although his character is fully drawn, there is little in it which indicates either the condition of the navy or the lieutenant's reactions to any specific phase of it. Thus, it is from John Jackson, who has served as surgeon's second mate on board of a seventy-gun ship, that Random learns of the wholesale bribery practiced in the navy offices, an evil which is frequently mentioned in the novel. Nothing can be accomplished, according to the worldly young Jackson, by the aspirant for any office or rank, without giving bribes; and this is the keynote of Roderick's own later experience with navy officials ashore. That this condition existed we have ample proof from Smollett's contemporaries,

---

[1] In *Life of Tobias George Smollett* (London, 1887), chap. 2.

as well as in the work of later students.[2] Jackson tells Random that,

... after he [Jackson] had waited at the Navy office many months for a warrant to no purpose, he was fain to pawn some of his clothes, which raised a small sum, wherewith he bribed the secretary, who soon procured a warrant for him, notwithstanding he had affirmed the same day, that there was not one vacancy.[3]

Later Smollett tells of

... the command of the Lizard [20 guns] given to a man turned of fourscore, who had been lieutenant, since the reign of King William, and, notwithstanding his long service, would have probably died in that station, had he not applied some prize-money he had lately received to make interest with his superiors.[4]

Random goes to the navy office and files application for an order for examination at Surgeon's Hall. Here he learns from Jackson

... that being destitute of all means to equip himself for sea, when he [Jackson] received his last warrant, he had been recommended to a person who lent him a little money, after he had signed a will and power, entitling that person to lift his wages when they should become due, as also to inherit his effects in case of his death. That he was still under the tutorage and direction of that gentleman, who advanced him small sums from time to time upon his security, at the rate of 50 per cent.[5]

This seems unconscionable interest to us, but was considered not unreasonable in Smollett's day. The sailor was perpetually in the hands of these brokers because of the inefficient method of "pay-

---

[2] Namier bears witness that interest of some kind was necessary: ". . . of the two 'golden rules' which governed the services, 'interest and seniority,' the former was infinitely the more important. . . . 'what interest has he?' was the foremost question in the eighteenth century." *The Structure of Politics at the Accession of George* III (London, 1929), I, 36–37.

[3] Chap. 15. All references to, and excerpts from, Smollett's writings are, unless otherwise stated, taken from *The Works of Tobias Smollett,* 12 vols., Westminster, 1899–1901.

[4] Chap. 36. In Thompson's revision of Shadwell's *Fair Quaker of Deal,* London, 1775, pp. 3–4, a captain of the navy is told: "Had you as much interest with the first lord of the admiralty, you might have a broad pennant, and sail around the world a dozen times." Thompson refers to Anson.

[5] Chap. 16.

ing off" then used. Instead of cash, he received a "ticket," sup-
posedly redeemable at face value. The custom, however, was to
sell these notes at a high rate of discount; for example, when
Roderick receives his pay from the *Thunder* in Jamaica, he sells
his ticket to a "Jew" at the rate of 40 per cent.[6] It is interesting that
Smollett himself granted power of attorney to a James Henshaw,
to receive the £38 5s. 11d. due after the novelist's service on the
Chichester.[7]

At the navy office Random is called before the board and ques-
tioned about his birthplace and education. He receives a letter to
Surgeon's Hall, where he has to pay a shilling to have the clerk
enter his name on the books; after waiting two weeks he is called
for examination. He says that he was led, trembling with fright,

> ... into a large hall, where I saw about a dozen of grim faces sitting at
> a long table, one of whom bade me come forward.... The first ques-
> tion he put to me was, "Where was you born?" To which I answered,—
> "in Scotland."—"In Scotland," said he, "I know that very well; we
> have scarce any other country men to examine here; you Scotchmen
> have overspread us of late as the locusts did Egypt..."[8] A plump
> gentleman who sat opposite to me, with a skull before him ... exam-
> ined me touching the operation of the trepan, and was very well satis-
> fied with my answers. The next person who questioned me was a
> wag ... "If ... during an engagement at sea, a man should be brought
> to you with his head shot off, how would you behave?" ... he desired
> me to advance to the gentlemen who sat next him, and who, with a
> pert air, asked what method of cure I would follow in wounds of the
> intestines. I repeated the method of cure as it is prescribed by the best
> chirurigical writers ... he stopped me, by saying, with some precipita-
> tion, "... I affirm, that all wounds of the intestines, whether great or
> small, are mortal."—"Pardon me, brother," says the fat gentleman,
> "there is very good authority"—here he was interrupted by the other
> with "Sir, excuse me, I despise all authority, *Nullius in verba*. I stand

---

[6] Chap. 35.

[7] For this information we are indebted to W. G. Perrin, "Tobias George Smollett," *The Mariner's Mirror*, X (Jan., 1924), 94.

[8] Previously (chap. 15) Random has been warned by Cringer, a Member of Parliament, that the medical branch of the navy was overrun with Scots.

upon my own bottom." "But, sir, sir," replied his antagonist, "the reason of the thing shows"—"A fig for reason," cried this sufficient member, "I laugh at reason, give me ocular demonstration."[9]

When Roderick receives his qualifications, he is ordered to pay five shillings:

I laid down my half-guinea upon the table, and stood some time, until one of them [the examiners] bade me begone. To this, I replied, "I will, when I have got my change,"... another threw me five shillings and six pence, saying, I would not be a true Scotchman if I went away without my change. I was afterwards obliged to give three shillings and sixpence to the beadles, and a shilling to an old woman who swept the hall.[10]

He goes to the navy office the following day and learns that he is qualified for a second surgeon's mate on a third rate. There are no prospects of an appointment, however, because his purse has been emptied and he cannot afford the necessary "presents." There can be little doubt that the account of Random's experience at the navy office and Surgeon's Hall agrees, in the main, with that of the author and, possibly, of Goldsmith, who failed the examination for surgeon's mate nineteen years after Smollett passed.[11] In one interesting detail, however, Smollett was much more fortunate than Random. The novelist was "granted a war-

---

[9] Chap. 17. For the general relationship of Smollett with medicine, see my edition of *An Essay on the External Use of Water* (Baltimore, 1935), pp. 31–50; and my "Tobias Smollett on the 'Separation of the Pubic Joint in Pregnancy,'" *Medical Life*, XLI (1934), 302–305. The latter article is a discussion and reprint of the "Observation" referred to below. The question involved was one that was to decide the fate of the study of medicine. Not only the quacks, with whom London and Bath were infested, but respectable medical practitioners as well, still clung tightly to the skirts of tradition and authority. Smollett, in his *Essay on the External Use of Water,* in the "Observation," and throughout his other writing on contemporary medicine, shows that he did not belong to this class. He, in the words of the famous surgeon Samuel Sharp, found that "in the practice of Physic it is often exceedingly difficult to ascertain a Fact" (*A Critical Enquiry into the Present State of Surgery* [London, 1754], p. 269). This quality of original observation, coupled with lack of diplomacy, was probably responsible for Smollett's failure as a medical practitioner, but it is one of the chief factors contributing to his success with the realistic novel.

[10] Chap. 17.

[11] [Anon.], "Dr. Oliver Goldsmith," *New York Medical Journal*, CXII (Nov., 1920), 727–728; Goldsmith, *Collected Letters,* ed. K. Balderston (Cambridge [Eng.], 1928), p. xxx.

rant by the Navy Board authorizing him to serve as a Surgeon's Mate in a Third Rate Ship of the line"[12] on March 10, 1740, and on April 3 he "was entered in H.M.S. *Chichester* in that capacity." Evidently Smollett managed to raise the "present."

Random's money is completely exhausted while he waits for an appointment, and he is forced to seek employment elsewhere. After many vicissitudes, he is seized by a press gang while on his way to see a friend at Wapping. His experience, which is similar to that of other pressed men, is as follows:

... as I crossed Tower-wharf, a squat tawny fellow, with a hanger by his side, and a cudgel in his hand, came up to me, calling, "Yo, ho! Brother, you must come along with me!" As I did not like his appearance, instead of answering his salutation, I quickened my pace, in hope of ridding myself of his company; upon which he whistled aloud, and immediately another sailor appeared before me, who laid hold of me by the collar, and began to drag me along. Not being of a humour to relish such treatment, I disengaged myself of the assailant, and, with one blow of my cudgel, laid him motionless on the ground; and perceiving myself surrounded in a trice, by ten or a dozen more, exerted myself with such dexterity and success, that some of my opponents were fain to attack me with drawn cutlasses; and, after an obstinate engagement, in which I received a large wound on my head, and another on my left cheek, I was disarmed, taken prisoner, and carried on board a pressing tender, where, after being pinioned like a malefactor, I was thrust down into the hold among a parcel of miserable wretches, the sight of whom well nigh distracted me.[13]

Roderick is robbed by one of his fellow prisoners, refused assistance by the midshipman on watch, and finally faints from loss of blood and "the noisesome stench of the place." The sailor who "rouses him out" brings a can of "flip," a beer drink so famous in the navy at the time, that Ironsides, a sailor in Richard Cumberland's *Brothers,* says, "Flip and tobacco is the only luxury we have any relish for ..."[14] Ironsides' other luxury, chewing tobacco, was much used before the advent of steamships because of the

---

[12] Perrin, *op. cit.*
[13] Chap. 24.
[14] In Mrs. Inchbald's *British Theatre* (London, 1808), XVIII, 16.

rigid restrictions placed on smoking in wooden ships; and Lieutenant Bowling always carries tobacco, "... of which he constantly chewed a large quid." Edward Thompson in his *Seaman's Letters,* says that in "the last war [that of Jenkyns' Ear] a chew of tobacco, a rattan, and a rope of oaths were sufficient qualifications to constitute a lieutenant."[15]

The day after Random is pressed, he is put aboard the *Thunder,* an eighty-gun ship. Smollett, like his hero, served in a third rate, and in the *Account* he says truly that he was aboard "one of the largest ships in the fleet,"[16] which did not contain any vessels of more than eighty guns. Just how true to life the crew of the *Thunder* are, we cannot tell, although it may well be that few if any of the many personalities aboard Random's ship coincided exactly with the personnel of the *Chichester*.

Once aboard the *Thunder,* Random is made "server" (orderly) to the surgeon's mates. Fortunately for him, the third mate has just died, and he is assigned to that place. The ship's surgeon six weeks later succeeds in having Roderick's appointment confirmed by the navy office so that, despite the inauspicious manner in which he enters the service, he ranks almost as high as his qualifications allow. The cockpit, where the surgeon's mates have their quarters, is described as follows:

We descended by divers ladders to a space as dark as a dungeon, which I understood was immersed several feet under water, being immediately above the hold. I had no sooner approached this dismal gulph, than my nose was saluted with an intolerable stench of putrified cheese and rancid butter, that issued from an apartment at the foot of the ladder, resembling a chandler's shop ... taking a light in his hand, [Thomson] conducted me to the place of his residence, which was a square of about six feet, surrounded with a medicine chest, that of the first mate, his own, and a board, by way of a table fastened to the after-powder room; it was also inclosed with canvas nailed round to the beams of the ship; to screen us from the cold, as well as from the view of the midshipmen and quartermasters, who lodged within the cable tiers on each side of us.[17]

<hr>

[15] London, 1756, p. 83.   [16] *Works,* XII, 191.   [17] Chap. 24.

Thomson regales the new man with some "cold salt pork ... and
... a can of beer, of which he made excellent flip." Random learns
later that it is "banyan day," and the first regular meal he has
aboard is described as follows:

... we heard the boatswain pipe to dinner; and immediately the boy
belonging to our mess ran to the locker, from whence he carried off a
large wooden platter, and in a few minutes returned with it full of
boiled peas, crying "Scaldings," all the way as he came. The cloth,
consisting of a piece of an old sail, was instantly laid, covered with
three plates, which, by their colour, I could with difficulty discern to
be metal, and as many spoons of the same composition, two of which
were curtailed in the handles, and the other abridged in the lip. Mr.
Morgan himself enriched this mess with a lump of salt butter, scooped
from an old gallipot, and a handfull of onions shorn, with some
pounded pepper.[18]

On the following day, Mr. Morgan, surgeon's first mate,

... ordering the boy to bring a piece of salt beef from the brine, cut
off a slice, and mixed it with an equal quantity of onions, which, sea-
soning with a moderate proportion of pepper and salt, he brought it
into a consistence with oil and vinegar: ... assured us it was the best
salmagundy that he ever made ...[19]

It is difficult for the twentieth-century reader to realize the
monotony of the diet on a ship which carried no ice: the only
vegetables to be had were onions and dried peas; salt pork and
salt beef, with dried fish, formed the staple fare four days a week;
hard biscuit took the place of bread; butter and cheese completed
the menu. In the time of Elizabeth, the seaman's diet consisted
of beer, biscuit, salt beef or salt pork with peas, salt fish, butter,
and cheese.[20] Pepys, in his *Diary,* speaks of "ships diet ... some
pease and pork,"[21] and Head, writing in the seventeenth century,
mentions "... beef and pork (that stirred as if it had received

---

[18] Chap. 25.
[19] Chap. 26. Commander Charles Robinson writes, as late as 1909, that "the salt and
pungent salmagundy, the potent and spicy bumbo are both known to us." See Charles
Robinson and John Leyland, *The British Tar in Fact and Fiction* (London, 1909), p. 269.
[20] Cyprian Bridge, "Did Elizabeth Starve Her Seamen?" *Nineteenth Century,* L. (Nov.,
1901), 779.
[21] Wheatley's ed. (London, 1924), p. 149.

second life and was crawling out of the platter to seek out the rest of his members)."[22]

What happened to this type of provision after some time in the tropics is well described by Smollett:

... our provision consisted of putrid salt beef to which the sailors gave the name of Irish horse; salt pork of New England, which, though neither fish nor flesh, savoured of both; bread from the same country, every biscuit whereof, like a piece of clock-work, moved by its own internal impulse, occasioned by the myriads of insects that dwelt within it; and butter served out by the gill, that tasted like train oil thickened with salt.[23]

This situation probably accounts for the 1,895 pounds of cheese which Lieutenant Watkins condemned aboard the *Chichester* on December 22, 1740.[24] In the *Account*[25] Smollett speaks of "putrid beef, rusty pork, and bread swarming with maggots." Anson, before he left for the South Seas, reported to the Admiralty that, in hot climates, "the Pease and Oatmeal put on board his Majty. Ships have generally decayed and become not fit to issue."[26] Poor food was not, however, limited to British ships, for we learn, from the *Voyage,* that aboard a Spanish man-of-war, "rats, when they could be caught, were sold for five dollars a piece..."[27]

Water became an important item in the tropics. In *Roderick Random,* Smollett says of the bombardment of the forts of Boca Chica and Saint Joseph,

... of all the consequences of the victory, none was more grateful than plenty of fresh water, after we had languished five weeks on an allowance of a purser's quart *per diem* for each man, in the Torrid Zone, where the sun was vertical, and the expence of bodily fluid so great, that a gallon of liquor could scarce supply the waste of twenty-four hours....[28]

[22] Richard Head and Francis Kirkman, *The English Rogue* (New York, 1928), p. 244.
[23] Chap. 33.
[24] See p. 39, *supra.*
[25] *Works,* XII, 206.
[26] Masefield's introduction to Walter's *Voyage,* p. iv.
[27] *Ibid.,* p. 30.
[28] Chap. 33.

In the *Account* the matter is treated in much the same way:

... the people on board of the fleet, who had been hitherto restricted to a very scanty allowance of this element, namely a purser's quart (about three half pints) per diem to every individual: in a climate where ... as many gallons might have been necessary to repair the waste of four and twenty hours, in a hard working man, sweating under the sun, which was vertical....[29]

When water was finally brought on board, however,

... in some ships so little pains had been taken to cleanse the vessels, that the water was corrupted, and stunk so abominably, that a man was fain to stop his nose with one hand, while with the other he conveyed the can to his head.[30]

Admiral Vernon, whose nickname was "Old Grog," originated the drink that came to be named after him. Smollett describes it as follows:

Instead of small beer [which soured in warm climates], each man was allowed three half-quarterns of brandy or rum, which were distributed every morning, diluted with a certain quantity of his water, without either sugar or fruit to render it palatable; for which reason, this composition was, by the sailors, not unaptly, styled *Necessity.*[31]

In the *Account* he refers to it as "... a most unpalatable drench, which no man could swallow without reluctance."[32]

The most vivid section of Smollett's treatment of the navy is his description of the sick bay aboard the *Thunder:*

... when I followed him [i.e. Thomson] with the medicines into the sick berth or hospital and observed the situation of the patients, I was much less surprised that people should die on board, than that any sick person should recover. Here I saw about fifty miserable distempered wretches, suspended in rows, so huddled upon one another, that not more than fourteen inches space was allotted for each, with his bed and bedding; and deprived of the light of day, as well as of fresh air; breathing nothing but a noisesome atmosphere of the morbid

---

[29] This and the following quotation are from *Works,* XII, 206.
[30] *Ibid.* This resembles Head's "water that stunk (as if stercus humanum had been steeped two or three days in it)." *The English Rogue,* p. 244.
[31] *Roderick Random,* chap. 33.
[32] *Works,* XII, 207.

steams exhaling from their own excrements and diseased bodies, devoured with vermin hatched in the filth that surrounded them, and destitute of every convenience necessary for people in that helpless condition.[33]

The duties of a "dresser" were arduous, and required practice, as Roderick soon discovered. The work was complicated by the presence of vermin, and when Thomson went to work he was seen to

... thrust his wig into his pocket, and strip himself to his waistcoat ..., creep on all fours under the hammocks of the sick, and, forcing up his bare pate between two, keep them asunder with one shoulder until he had done his duty.[34]

Roderick, on his return to the cockpit, found that

... some guests had honoured me with their company, whose visit I did not at all think seasonable ... I took the advice of my friend, who, to prevent such misfortunes, went always close shaved.

Finally, the *Thunderer* leaves for the West Indies, and, during a storm, one of the sailors breaks his leg. Mackshane, the surgeon, orders amputation. When the mates disagree with him, he shifts the responsibility to them. Fortunately, they are successful; the fracture knits in six weeks.

The improvements in sterilization methods which have taken place since the days of Smollett make it hard for the modern reader to understand the frequency with which amputation was resorted to at that time. Charrière, one of the most famous of eighteenth-century French surgical writers, states that "... you must never wash wounds; it is sufficient to cleanse them with lint";[35] and his English successor, Dr. Sharp, observing that "the treatment of wounds ... seems to be fundamentally the same in

---

[33] Chap. 25.

[34] This and the following passage occur in chapter 26, where sick call is described: "At a certain hour in the morning, the boy of the mess went round all the decks, ringing a small hand-bell, and, in rhymes composed for the occasion, invited all those who had sores to repair before the mast, where one of the doctor's mates attended, with applications to dress them."

[35] *A Treatise on the Operation of Surgery* (London, 1712), p. 244.

every country in Europe,"[36] explains that "some of the most eminent Surgeons in England not only defer the Amputation till the
gangrene is stopt, but even till it is advanced in its Separation."
All wounds were extremely liable to gangrene, and it was usually
better to remove the limb than take a chance of losing the patient.
What happened when the operation was too long delayed is
shown by Oexmelin, buccaneer and doctor:

Deux jours apres la gangrene se mit a sa jambe, ensorte que je fus
obligé de la luy couper, depuis ses playes allerent for bein & nous par-
lions de ja de luy faire une jambe de bois, lors qu'en un nuit il luy vint
un erisiple a la jambe sane depuis la lance jusqu'au talon. Je le seignay,
le purgeay doucement, et tachay d'appaiser l'inflammation avec des
remedes convenables; cela n'empescha pas sa jambe de tomber en
pourriture, & quoyque je pusse faire, il mourut.[37]

Smollett's description of the cockpit during the action against
Boca Chica derives most of its interest rather from the actions,
heroic or extravagant, of the men who are there, than from the
place itself;[38] we find that the surgeons are independent of the
captain's authority during an engagement. Smollett devotes more
space in the *Account* to conditions aboard the hospital ships with
Vernon at Cartagena:

As for the sick and wounded, they were next day sent on board of the
transports and vessels called hospital-ships, where they languished
in want of every necessary comfort and accommodation. They were
destitute of surgeons, nurses, cooks, and proper provision; they were
pent up between decks in small vessels, where they had not room to
sit upright; they wallowed in filth; myriads of maggots were hatched
in the putrifaction of their sores, which had no other dressing than
that of being washed by themselves with their own allowance of
brandy; and nothing was heard but groans and lamentations, and the
language of despair invoking death to deliver them from their mis-
eries. What served to encourage this despondency, was the prospect
of the poor wretches who had strength and opportunity to look around

---

[36] *Critical Enquiry,* preface. The following quotation is from p. 276.

[37] *Histoire des Avanturiers* (Paris, 1688), pp. 229–230.

[38] Ward describes the cockpit as an "Infernal Region of his [i.e. the surgeon's] ... a
bloody place, that's the truth on't, and dark enough to hide all his Miscarriages." *Wooden
World Dissected* (London, 1929), p. 64.

them; for there they beheld the naked bodies of their fellow-soldiers and comrades floating up and down the harbour, affording prey to the carrion crows and sharks, which tore them in pieces without interruption, and contributed by their stench to the mortality that prevailed.... Every ship of war in the fleet could have spared a couple of surgeons for their relief; and many young gentlemen of that profession solicitated their captains in vain for leave to go and administer help to the sick and wounded.[39]

With the campaign itself, the battles and mistakes, we are not directly concerned. Smollett is, of course, extremely critical, as he may well have been. Perhaps this explains the feeling of some navy men that he is an unsympathetic outsider as far as his criticism of the service is concerned. Like Carlyle, he never seems to disassociate entirely the mob from the individuals of whom it is composed. Hence, none of his pictures vary much from his customary portraits, each posed against a background cluttered with the debris of his environment. That the creator of Oakum and Whiffle became disgusted with a service that degraded and brutalized a man as soon as he entered it, is small cause for exclamation. How he could have reacted in any other way to the navy as he found it, is incomprehensible, yet he is never such a snob as Anson's chaplain, Dr. Walter, occasionally shows himself to be. For Smollett did not think the less of a man, as a human being, because he was dirty or of low station. Nowhere is this more important than in his treatment of the British sailor, whose actual background offers so vivid an excuse for whatever irrationality the author may be said to display.

Smollett's Nautical Characters

The nautical characters treated by Smollett fall, roughly, into three groups: those whom he actually knew, those who appear in his journalistic or historical work, and those of his own cre-

---

[39] *Works,* XII, 216–217. Fortescue and other historians of this campaign substantiate this picture; many of them quote Smollett directly, or copy his work.

ation. That there are occasional ties binding the first two classes with the third is apparent. As it is impossible, however, except in a very few cases, to say definitely whom he did know personally, we must confine the first class to those two officers who appear in his letters as his personal friends.

The first of these is a Captain Mann, who had sailed around the world with Anson,[1] and who was to become Rear Admiral of the Red in 1770.[2] Mr. Noyes, editor of the *Letters,* thinks[3] that he may have been the original of the officer in *Humphrey Clinker:* "A captain of a man of war, who had made the circuit of the globe with Mr. Anson, being conducted to this glen [Cameron on Leven, Scotland] exclaimed,—'Juan Fernandez, by God!'"[4] The other, Lieutenant Robert Love, is obscure, though Smollett vouches "for his being a brave, honest, and skillful mariner."[5] The author speaks of both men with marked kindness, recommending them to his acquaintances in Glasgow as friends of long standing.

During the course of his career as literary critic and political journalist, Smollett had many opportunities to comment on navy officers. Most of his criticism is harsh, by our standards, occasionally sinking to downright scurrility. For example, the criticism which he directed against Admiral Knowles in the *Critical Review* resulted in the author's imprisonment for three months. Knowles, a captain in 1741, commanded the *Weymouth* (60 guns) in the Cartagena expedition, where Smollet may have heard of him from members of his crew. The admiral seems to have been a disagreeable person, whose naval career was spotted

---

[1] *Letters of Tobias Smollett,* Edward S. Noyes, ed. (Cambridge [Mass.], 1926), p. 46. This volume will be referred to as *Letters* hereafter.

[2] Mann was captain of the *Anson* (60 guns) in February, 1755 (see *Scots Mag.,* XVII, 109, 161). In April, 1757, he became commander of the *Porcupine* (*ibid.,* XXIX, 220). On October 18, 1770, he was made Rear Admiral of the Blue (*ibid.,* XXXII, 576), and six days later, of the Red (*ibid*).

[3] *Letters,* p. 161.

[4] *Works,* IV, 122.

[5] *Letters,* pp. 70–71.

with court-martial and official reprimand,[6] and it is probable that Smollett's comments were doubly disagreeable because they contained more than a hint of truth.[7]

Of Admiral Vernon and his confrere at Cartagena, General Wentworth, Smollett is also extremely critical. In *Roderick Random* he ridicules both men,[8] continuing in the same vein eight years later in the *Account,*[9] as well as in the *History.*[10] Byng, on the other hand, is handled in more kindly fashion in Smollett's private correspondence,[11] in the *Critical Review,*[12] and in his *History.*[13] It must be remembered, however, that Smollett might well have been affected by two considerations; first, he was not forced to endure any personal hardship because of Byng's mistakes, as he was because of the disagreement between Vernon and Wentworth; second, Lord Bute's adherents were fighting the existing administration tooth and nail, a fact which gave the author a definite political reason for kindness to a "victim" of the party in power. This, of course, makes his treatment of the government's neglect of Knowles doubly important, as one would expect the enemies of the Duke of Newcastle, of whom the author of *Adventures of an Atom*[14] was certainly one, to see the matter through eyes prejudiced in favor of the admiral.

Lord Anson receives little kindness from Smollett. He is slightingly referred to in the *History,*[15] and in the *Adventures of an Atom,* under the name of "Ninkom-poo-po," he is the object of partisan ridicule, his voyage around the world reduced to farcical buffoonery. It is not surprising that Anson and his reforms should

---

[6] Arnold Whitridge, *Tobias Smollett* ([New York], 1925), p. 38 n.; John Entick, *A New Naval History* (London, 1757), pp. 820–821; Smollett, *The History of England from the Revolution to the Death of George II* (London, 1807), IV, 67–70.
[7] See Appendix A.
[8] Chap. 33.
[9] *Works,* XII, 211–212.
[10] III, 58–61.
[11] *Letters,* p. 39.
[12] See II (Oct., 1756), 252, 257, (Nov.), 286; III (Feb., 1757), 185, (March), 238.
[13] IV, 80–81.
[14] *Works,* XII, 224–433. In the *Adventures,* Newcastle is called "Fika-kaka."
[15] III, 141–143.

have been subject to ridicule and hostility when he became First Lord of the Admiralty, but it is regrettable that Smollett, whose sympathy toward the seaman was keen, should have permitted himself to write scoffingly of one who was ever popular with his inferiors, as Anson seems to have been.

It is the seamen who enter Smollett's novels and farce, however, with whom we are most concerned in this study. In his capacity of surgeon's mate, the author was, although rated as an officer, the inferior of the other officers. His medical duties gave him an excellent opportunity to come in close contact with the sailors, to observe them, and to gain a fair knowledge of their life aboard ship. He seldom treats the actual routine of sailorcraft, however, except so far as it must have affected him personally. But his insight into the character and psychology of the "man before the mast" and the deck officer makes him the first, and still one of the best, portrayers of the living English sailor.

Smollett's fictional marine characters may be divided conveniently according to their rating in the service. This will not necessitate separate consideration of merchant seamen, who are not of sufficient importance to receive lengthy treatment. In Smollett's work, as in the navy itself, the officers fall into two classes: the gentlemen, and the "tarpawlins," those who obtained commissions after sailing as seamen. These classes are not mutually exclusive, as Captain Oakum and Surgeon's First Mate Morgan prove, but they are sufficiently well marked for the present purpose. Where elements distinguishing both groups enter the character of a single individual, he will be assigned arbitrarily to the class in which the sum of his characteristics would seem to place him.

Captain Oakum, Random's commanding officer on the *Thunder* during the Cartagena expedition, is the most clearly portrayed man of his rank to be found in the author's gallery of naval characters. He typifies the brutality, not only of the service at that time, but of the century as a whole. From the time when the reader is introduced to him, in Lieutenant Bowling's letter,[16] until the rearrival of the fleet at Jamaica, after the Cartagena fiasco, where the captain is transferred to another ship,[17] Oakum is coarse, ignorant, inhuman, aloof from crew and fellow officers alike, susceptible to flattery but oblivious to the dictates of humanity.

His assault on Lieutenant Bowling is briefly treated in that officer's letter to Mr. Potion, a Glasgow doctor to whom the young Random is apprenticed:

...I have quitted the Thunder man of war, being obliged to sheer off, for killing my captain.... And I would serve the best man so that ever stept between stem and stern, if so be that he struck me, as Captain Oakum did.[18]

Unfortunately, the lieutenant's assumption that the captain is dead proves to be erroneous. Roderick later meets Jack Rattlin, who was a sailor on the *Thunder* when the encounter took place, and learns the truth:

Now we lying at anchor in Tuberroon [Tiberoon] bay, Lieutenant Bowling had the middle watch, and as he always kept a good look out, he made, d'ye see, three lights in the offing, whereby he ran down to the cabin for orders, and found the Captain asleep; whereupon he waked him, which put him in a main high passion, and he swore woundily at the lieutenant, and called him a lousy Scotch son of a whore (for I being then centinel in the steerage, heard all), and swab and lubber, whereby the lieutenant returned the salute, and they jawed together, fore and aft, a good spell, till at last the captain turned out, and laying hold of a rattan, came athwart Mr. Bowling's quarter; whereby he told the captain, that, if he was not his commander he would have him overboard, and demanded satisfaction ashore; whereby, in the morning watch the captain went ashore in the pinnace, and afterwards the lieutenant carried the cutter ashore; and so they, leaving the boats' crews on their oars, went away together; and so, d'ye see, in less than a quarter of an hour, we heard firing, whereby we

---

[16] Chap. 6.
[17] Chap. 34.
[18] Chap. 6.

made for the place, and found the captain lying wounded on the beach, and so brought him on board to the doctor, who cured him in less than six weeks. But the lieutenant clapped on all the sail he could bear, and had got far enough ahead before we knew anything of the matter; so that we could never after get sight of him, for which we were not sorry, because the captain was mainly wroth, and would certainly have done him a mischief; for he afterwards caused him to be run on the ship's books, whereby he lost all his pay, and if he should be taken, would be tried as a deserter.[19]

This incident affords an excellent example of Oakum's treatment of his brother officers, as well as of his vindictiveness. Later, one of the main sources of contention at the time is touched on when Rattlin explains that the captain is "lord, or baron knight's brother, whereby d'ye see me, he carries a straight arm, and keeps aloof from his officers, tho', may hap, they may be as good men in the main as he."

Rattlin's is truly a sailor's viewpoint. In Shadwell's *Fair Quaker of Deal,* for example, Commodore Flip says:

...I say the best officers that ever saw salt-water, and not a drop of nobility in them....I know no man that is a gentleman,—or that can be one,—who has not been to sea and is a sailor...."[20]

As early as the seventeenth century the anonymous author of the *Reflections on Navall Discipline* speaks of the "animosities in the Fleet" springing "from this distinction of Gentleman and Tarpaulin."[21] After Charles II offered opportunity and encouragement to those of gentle blood to enter the service, there were many instances of the "tarpawlin's" animosity toward the gentleman officer, who usually had influence ashore.

Random has been aboard the *Thunder* six weeks when Oakum comes aboard. The captain's first act after his arrival is the most callously brutal to be found in any of Smollett's work. When

---

[19] This and the following quotation are taken from chap. 24.

[20] Thompson's revision, p. 5.

[21] [1685–1690?] MS in New York Public Library. And see the pride in seamanship which causes the Master and Sailor to deride scholarship in Lodge's *Looking Glass for London and England*.

Morgan presents the sick list, the commander cries, "Blood and oons! sixty-one sick people on board of my ship! Hark 'ee, you sir, I'll have no sick in my ship, by God."[22] He orders all the sick to muster on the quarterdeck. The inhumanity of this order is apparent as they drag themselves up from the sick bay, but the surgeon will not, and the mates cannot, protest. When the muster is complete, the captain bids the doctor,

... who stood bowing at his right hand, look at these lazy lubberly sons of bitches who was good for nothing on board but to eat the king's provision, and encourage idleness in the skulkers.

As the men are examined, one by one, the surgeon puts them back to work. One dies the next day; another is "suffocated with a deluge of blood issuing from his lungs" when made to man the pump; a third, whipped into the rigging, falls into the water. Of the original sixty-one, less than a dozen remain alive. When the last, a madman, is freed he can scarcely be prevented from murdering both captain and surgeon before he is secured.

Soon after the *Thunder* enters the warm latitudes, Random and Morgan are seized and pinioned to the deck of the poop. Roderick remains there "exposed to the scorching heat of the sun by day, and to the unwholesome damps by night" for twelve days, without trial or examination. During this time an action in which the *Thunder* is involved is fought with some French men-of-war, and the surgeon's second mate is forced to witness it, helpless in his chains. When the fleet nears Jamaica, however, the captain, fearing the results of a court-martial, holds a court of his own. During the trial he storms, threatens, displays his own ignorance, and finally remands Random and Morgan to irons. They are released only when the two perjured witnesses, on whose testimony the surgeon's mates have been convicted as spies, quarrel and blurt out the truth.

The only relief in the blackness of Oakum's character is

---

[22] This and the following quotation are taken from chap. 27.

afforded by his conduct during the storming of Boca Chica. Here he is shown to possess the calm presence of mind, in the face of danger, so necessary to a leader in active service. But his later brutality in refusing to permit the fever-stricken Random to change berths when confinement in the sick bay or surgeon's mates' quarters means sure death, leaves the reader with the impression of the captain gained from his first muster of the sick.

It has been customary for critics to consider Oakum as a caricature, an impossibly inhuman monster, with little foundation in actual fact. Such men did exist in the service, however, both before and after this period, as well as in the 1740's. Mr. David Hannay, in *The Life of Marryatt,* quotes the following entry from the private journal of Sir George Rooke:

This morning received information that Capt. Moses of the Melford had been attempted to be assassinated, and was shot in the leg. Upon which ordered Sir Jno. Minden to go aboard that ship with the Judge-advocate, Capt. Gifford, and Capt. Leake to enquire thereinto, which they having done by the best examination they could make, found upon the oaths of the officers, and the circumstances, that he was shot by himself, and, as supposed, was done on purpose to strengthen his case against Mr. Stucley his lieutenant, and Mr. Brookes, his midshipman extra, whom he had confined for above six months.[23]

The treatment of Mr. Brookes during his captivity was extremely brutal. Marryatt, himself, writing ninety years after the appearance of Smollett's first novel, *Roderick Random,* says of the mid-eighteenth century,

A combination of all that was revolting to humanity was practised, without any notice being taken of it by the superior powers, provided that the commanders of the vessels did their duty when called upon, and showed the necessary talent and courage.[24]

The commander who takes Oakum's place aboard the *Thunder* is the exact opposite of his predecessor, except in high-handed

---

[23] Entries for July 10 and 18, 1801; quoted in *Life of Frederick Marryatt* (London, 1889), p. 241.
[24] *Snarleyow* (London, 1897), chap. 3.

treatment of his inferiors. Captain Whiffle is an example of the sea-fop, of whom much was written both before and after this time. That such officers existed, there is ample proof. Callender, who is, as a rule, very kind in his treatment of naval officers, says that Whiffle "is borne out by an authoritative writer,"[25] while Shadwell presents the same type in Beau Mizen, who forms a foil for Flip, in the *Fair Quaker,* as Whiffle does for Oakum.

The new commander, who comes aboard the *Thunder* in a ten-oar barge, "overshadowed with a vast umbrella," is described as:

... a tall, thin, young man, dressed in this manner:—A white hat, garnished with a red feather, adorned his head, from whence his hair flowed upon his shoulders, in ringlets, tied behind with a ribbon. His coat, consisting of pink-coloured silk lined with white, by the elegance of the cut retired backward, as it were to discover a white satin waistcoat embroidered with gold, unbuttoned at the upper part to display a brooch set with garnets, that glittered in the breast of his shirt, which was of the finest cambric, edged with right Mechlin. The knees of his crimson velvet breeches scarcely descended so low as to meet his silk stockings, which rose without spot or wrinkle on his meagre legs, from shoes of blue Meroquin, studded with diamond buckles, that flamed forth rivals to the sun! A steel-hilted sword, inlaid with gold, and decked with a knot of ribbon which fell down in a rich tassel, equipped his side; and an amber-headed cane hung dangling from his wrist. But the most remarkable parts of his furniture were, a mask on his face, and white gloves on his hands, which did not appear to be put on with an intention to be pulled off occasionally, but were fixed with a curious ring on the little finger of each hand. In this garb Captain Whiffle (for that was his name) took possession of the ship, surrounded with a crowd of attendants, all of whom, in their different degrees, seemed to be of their patron's disposition; and the air was so impregnated with perfumes, that one may venture to affirm the clime of Arabia Felix was not half so sweet-scented.[26]

In Shadwell's play, the first thing Mizen does ashore is to send a sailor "... to the perfumers for the essence of the odour of roses, the violet-powder, the scented pomatum, the bergamot, and

---

[25] *Sea Kings of Britain—Albemarle to Hawke* (London, 1909), p. 150 n. Unfortunately, Callender does not name his source.
[26] Chap. 34.

an alum paste for my hands."[27] Whiffle's objection to the smell of tobacco is paralleled in Mizen. Smollett, characteristically, goes further to accuse the new commander of "maintaining a correspondence with his surgeon not fit to be named."[28]

The third captain under whom Roderick serves is an old man[29] who is only remarkable for his ill-humor and the fact that he considers surgeons "unnecessary animals on board of a ship."[30] Crampley, who takes command when the oldster dies, will be treated later in his previous capacity of midshipman.[31]

The other important captain in Smollett's work is that quixotic "original," Captain Crowe, a merchantman. Despite the fullness with which he is portrayed, however, Crowe, like Commodore Trunnion in *Peregrine Pickle,* is almost purely caricature. The occasional flashes of courage, the good-heartedness, the peculiarity of conversation and manners, which mark both men, are rather conventional than individual. Captain Clewline, also, in *Sir Launcelot Greaves,* who, "previous to his commitment to prison, was a commander of a sloop of war, and bore the reputation of a gallant officer,"[32] is seen only during his incarceration; and although the deterioration of character which takes place in him during confinement would doubtless interest a student in psychology, Clewline is of no importance as a realistic sailor.

One of the most memorable of Smollett's nautical figures is Roderick's uncle, Lieutenant Tom Bowling,[33] who is described as "a strong built man, somewhat bandy-legged, with a neck like that of a bull, and a face which, you might easily perceive, had

---

[27] *Op. cit.,* p. 5.
[28] Chap. 34. Smollett also treats of sodomy in the first edition of *Peregrine Pickle* and in some of his poems.
[29] Chaps. 36 ff.
[30] Chap. 37.
[31] See *infra,* p. 68.
[32] Chap. 21.
[33] He is among the most fully portrayed, and best-loved, sailors in English literature. It is significant that the anonymous author of a farce entitled *The Volunteers or the Adventures of Roderick Random and his friend Strap* keeps only one of the seamen who appear in the novel—namely, Lieutenant Bowling. See Howard Buck, "A Roderick Random Play—1748," *MLN,* XLIII (Feb., 1928), 111–112.

withstood the most obstinate assaults of the weather."[34] He is dressed in

> ... a sailor's coat altered for him by the ship's tailor, a striped flannel jacket, a pair of red breeches, japanned with pitch, clean grey worsted stockings, large silver buckles that covered three-fourths of his shoes, a silver laced hat, whose crown overlooked the brims about an inch and a half, a black bob wig in buckle, a check shirt, a silk handkerchief, a hanger with a brass handle girded to his thigh by a tarnished laced belt ...

It must be remembered here, and also in the description of Whiffle, that there were no set uniforms in Smollett's navy; hence each man dressed according to his own taste and purse. Some commanders, like Commodore Trunnion,[35] dressed their boatmen alike; although when Anson reached China he was forced to outfit some of his sailors in "the regimentals of the marines"[36] to obtain a uniform appearance.

Lieutenant Bowling, "unacquainted with the ways of men in general, to which his education on board had kept him an utter stranger,"[37] resembles Crowe, who is "as little acquainted with the world as a suckling child."[38] This guilelessness is a typical component of the "humours" sailor from Jonson's contemporaries to Conrad. Another traditional feature is that the effect of the Lieutenant's idiom and sea customs is laughter-provoking. His sturdy championship of the boy, Roderick, however, and the honest disgust with which the pettiness and hypocrisy of landsmen affect him are refreshing as a wind off the sea's face; and his unconditional bluntness is like that of Captain Manly, in Wycherly's *Plain Dealer*. Bowling's treatment of the tyrannical schoolmaster[39] is typical of the eighteenth-century seaman, to whom a "round dozen" was, as we have seen, the usual punishment for offenses short of desertion and mutiny. His curt recital of the affair with

---

[34] This and the following passage occur in chap. 3.
[35] Cf. chap. 8 of *Peregrine Pickle*.
[36] Walter, *A Voyage Round the World ... by George Anson*, p. 329.
[37] Chap. 3.   [38] Chap. 1.   [39] Chap. 5.

Captain Oakum, his honest admission that the French "are very civil,"[40] and his faith in "his Majesty, who (God bless him) will not suffer an honest tar to be wronged" denote the stock British "heart of oak."

It is in Rattlin's description of him, however, that we see the seafaring Bowling most completely. The sailor calls his officer "a good seaman . . . as ever stepped upon forecastle,—and a brave fellow as ever crack'd biskit;—none of your Guinea pigs,—nor your fresh-water, wishy-washy, fair-weather fowls,"[41] but a man who was "very much beloved by the ship's company." We regret that we are unable to meet Ben Block, "the first man that taught him to hand, reef, and steer."

When Random meets his uncle in a French tavern, the latter, not recognizing the youth, is wary: "Avast there, friend; none of your tricks upon travellers; if you have any thing to say to me, do it above board; you need not be afraid of being overheard; here are none who understand our lingo."[42] This would seem to indicate that the lieutenant, for all his simplicity, was capable of taking care of himself. Once these simple sailormen are put into their own environment, be it afloat or in a waterfront dive, they become human beings, not the puppets they seem inland in uncongenial society. When Bowling realizes who the stranger really is, his first regret is that he is unable to assist "Rory" financially, although when the younger man offers him enough money for passage to England, it is only with the greatest difficulty that he can be persuaded to accept.

The lieutenant's description of the ladder by which he intends to raise Random to surgeon's first mate shows his naïveté:

For the beadle of the Admiralty is my good friend; and he and one of the under clerks are sworn brothers and that under clerk has a good deal to say with one of the upper clerks, who is very well known to the

---

[40] This and the following quotation are from chap. 6.
[41] This and the following two quotations are from chap. 24.
[42] This and the following two quotations are from chap. 41.

under secretary, who, upon his recommendation, I hope, will recommend my affair to the first secretary, and he again will speak to one of the lords in my behalf.[43]

The younger man, less sanguine, suggests that Bowling borrow enough money "to enable him to appear as he ought, and make a small present to the under secretary, who might possibly dispatch his business the sooner on that account."

Lieutenant Bowling's ability as commander in action is shown on his first voyage to Guinea in a letter-of-marque. His captain being killed, he takes command, sinks the enemy, and, later in the voyage, captures a merchantman which he brings safe to Ireland. On the second trip, when Roderick is with him as ship's surgeon, the ship is overtaken by a man-of-war flying the colors of France. The sailors aboard the merchantman, not relishing so unequal a contest, want to surrender immediately; but Bowling musters the crew aft and addresses them:

My lads, I am told you hang an asse—I have gone to sea thirty years man and boy and never saw English sailors afraid before. Mayhap you may think I want to expose you for the lucre of gain. Whosoever thinks so, thinks a damned lie, for my whole cargo is insured; so that, in case I should be taken, my loss will not be great. The enemy is stronger than we, to be sure. What then? have we not a chance for carrying away one of her masts, and so get clear of her? If we find her too hard for us, 'tis but striking at last. If any man is hurt in the engagement, I promise, on the word of an honest seaman, to make him recompence according to his loss. So now, you that are lazy, lubberly, cowardly dogs, get away, and skulk in the hold and breadroom; and you that are jolly boys, stand by me, and let us give one broadside for the honour of Old England.[44]

He convinces them, but fortunately the stranger is an English ship in disguise.

[43] The lieutenant's comment on religion is also typical: "No honest man would swerve from the principles in which he was bred, whether Turkish, Protestant, or Roman" (chap. 42). It is significant that Smollett, in *Ferdinand, Count Fathom,* gives one of the earliest sympathetic pictures of a Jew to be found in English literature. This is a moneylender who makes his appearance in chapter 47.

[44] Chap. 65.

The last glimpse we have of the lieutenant is at the time of his refusal to stay ashore even long enough to attend his nephew's wedding, "being resolved to try his fortune once more at sea."[45] Despite the fact that he has made enough money in the two previous trips to enable him to settle ashore, he must "go down to the sea again."

Before we take leave of Lieutenant Bowling, it is well to consider one of Smollett's characters who is close kin to Roderick's uncle, by type, if not by blood. This is Lyon, lieutenant in *The Reprisal*. Both officers have a sailor named Ben Block as tutor in sailorcraft. Lyon, like Bowling, says, "I was once taken by the French, who used me nobly."[46] Block's description of Lyon is much like that of Bowling given by Jack Rattlin:

... he's as brisk a seaman as ever greased a marlin-spike—I'll turn 'un adrift with e'er a he that reefed a foresail—a will fetch up his leeway with a set sail, as the saying is. ... I have stood by him with my blood— and my heart—and my liver, in all weathers—blow high—blow low.[47]

The lieutenant's threat to Block in the play is reminiscent of Bowling, "... I shall have you to the gangway, you drunken swab."[48] All in all, the men are surprisingly similar, and it seems probable that Smollett, realizing the success of his earlier character, modeled Lyon after him.

Lieutenant Hatchway, Commodore Trunnion's companion in *Peregrine Pickle,* is a fun-loving "heart of oak." His affection for the impish and irascible Perry, his loyalty to the youngster and the Commodore, are typical of the romanticized treatment of the English sailor so common at the end of the eighteenth and the beginning of the nineteenth century. Like Trunnion, however, he is of little value in a study of realism.

[45] Chap. 69.
[46] *Works*, XII, 161. For an account of the performances of this play in 1757, 1759, 1762, and 1771, see Dougald MacMillan, *Drury Lane Calendar (1747–1776)* (Oxford, 1938), p. 313.
[47] *Works*, XII, 160.
[48] *Ibid.*

As we should expect, some of the best of Smollett's seafaring characters are drawn from the ranks of the *Thunder*'s surgeons and their mates. Of these Morgan and Mackshane are the principals. The latter, who is surgeon under Oakum during the Cartagena campaign, has no virtue, like his commander's courage, to lighten his character. He is completely under the domination of his master, fawning on that worthy while attempting to discredit all those who serve under him in the cockpit. His acquiescence in Oakum's brutal treatment of the sick,[49] the maliciousness with which he attempts to effect a complete case for espionage against Morgan and Random, and his effrontery in supposing that the two mates would be easily reconciled to him after the hardships they had undergone in captivity are typical of the man. During the bombardment at Boca Chica, he is so cowed and terrified that he refuses duty, even though the command comes from Oakum himself. It is only after he has frequently consulted the brandy bottle, and his mates have threatened to report him for cowardice when the engagement is over, that Mackshane is of any use in the cockpit at all. Then the carelessness and ignorance which characterize him become manifest, and arms and legs are "hewed down without mercy."

This close connection between captain and surgeon seems to have been common enough in the navy of the time. In Anson's *Voyages* it is Mr. Elliott, surgeon aboard the *Wagar,* who stands by Captain Cheap after the crew of the wrecked vessel have taken matters pretty well into their own hands. In this connection, it must be remembered that the surgeon was extremely important in the days when ships were so long at sea. This was especially true of fighting ships—both naval and pirate vessels. On the latter, the surgeon was paid and his medical kit stocked before any prize money was shared among the rest of the crew. The surgeon was the only man aboard a pirate ship who did not have to sign the

---

[49] *Supra,* p. 57.

articles unless he so desired. Oexmelin was a surgeon, as were Thomas Dover[50] and Lionel Wafer. Captain Low, the pirate, although he usually exercised despotic power over his crew, inflicted no punishment on the surgeon who, when Low found fault with the way his mouth was sewed, smashed the captain with his fist, ripping out the stitches, with the advice, "Go to hell and sew up your own chops."[51] Something of this independent spirit is to be found in Morgan, surgeon's first mate aboard the *Thunder.*

The other chief surgeons to be found in Smollett are: Dr. Tomlins, the first man under whom Roderick serves, a kindly, intelligent man; Simper, Whiffle's personal doctor, who seems to have risen to that position chiefly because of sexual perversion and an effeminate "bedside manner"; and Mr. Fillet, in *Sir Launcelot Greaves,* who is only introduced to interpret the nautical idiom of Captain Crowe.

Among the surgeon's mates, Morgan is the most important. He is, however, rather a racial caricature than a convincing person. It has been frequently remarked that, for some of the Welshman's peculiarities, Smollett may well be indebted to the Fluellen of Shakespeare's *Henry V.* Morgan's behavior in his first meeting with Random is typical of the first mate, and also offers a good example of the author's technique of character presentation:

... we [i.e., Random and Thomson] heard a voice on the cockpit ladder pronounce with great vehemence, in a strange dialect, "The devil and his dam blow me from the top of Mounchdenny, if I go to him before there is something in my belly; let his nose be as yellow as saffron, or as plus as a pell, look you, or green as a leek, 'tis all one." To this declaration somebody answered, "... I see you don't mind what

[50] Cf. Philip Gosse, *The Pirates' Who's Who* (Boston, 1924); Oexmelin, *Histoire des Avanturiers;* William Osler, "Thomas Dover, M.D.," *Johns Hopkins Hospital Bulletin,* VII (1896), 1–6; L. Eloesser, "Pirate and Buccaneer Doctors," *Annals of Medical History,* VIII (March, 1926), 31–60; J. Nixon, "Further Notes on Thomas Dover," *Proceedings of the Royal Society of Medicine,* VI (May 29, 1913), 233–237. Thomas Lodge, the Elizabethan author, served aboard a privateer, but evidently did not study medicine until he had left the sea.
[51] Eloesser, *op. cit.,* p. 53.

your master says." Here he was interrupted with "Splunter and cons! get you gone to the doctor, and tell him my birth, and education, and abilities, and moreover my behaviour is as good as his, or any shentleman's (no disparagement to him) in the whole world. . . ." He was a short thick man, with a face garnished with pimples, a snubnose turned up at the end, an excessive wide mouth, and little fiery eyes, surrounded with skin puckered up in innumerable wrinkles.[52]

Morgan has an excessive admiration for pedigree, a stubborn pride, and an intense respect for Random's knowledge of medicine. When he is angered, not even regard for his own physical safety will influence him, as is shown by his answer to Oakum at the trial.

I spoke by metaphor, and parable, and comparison, and types; as we signify meekness by a lamb, lechery by a goat, and craftiness by a fox; so we liken ignorance to an ass, and brutality to a bear, and fury to a tiger; therefore I made use of these similes to express my sentiments, look you, and what I said before Got, I will not unsay before man or peast neither.[53]

With his friends, however, he is openhearted and good-natured. Despite the callous indifference which marks his attitude toward death in general, he is distracted with grief when he thinks Random is dead. Smollett, who is always apt to provide for the future of his main characters, finally settles Morgan as an apothecary in Canterbury.

Second Surgeon's Mate Thomson is, like Random, a Scot. He meets Roderick first at the navy office in London, befriends him when he is pressed, and acts as guide and advisor to the new man after he secures him the appointment as dresser and, later, as third mate. Until he attempts suicide, Thomson, Random's best friend, is a realistic character. Once he has jumped over the side of the *Thunder,* however, he becomes a most romantic figure: the young man is rescued at sea by a Scotch friend, then carried to Jamaica and introduced to a plantation owner who makes him overseer. Later, by chance, he meets Random again, which is not surpris-

[52] Chap. 25. [53] Chap. 30.

ing, since such fortuitous meetings are common in Smollett—
his heritage from the Greek novel.

Random's own character, as he first appears, is closer kin to
such a picaresque protagonist as Gil Blas than to the conventional
conception of a hero. Once at sea, however, Roderick becomes
much more human and decent. His panic in the action against
the French cannot be held against him when the reader reflects
that Random was chained helpless during the cannonading, that
the brains of a decapitated officer were splashed in his face, and
a dead body flung across him. Later, in the bombardment at Boca
Chica, he shows that he is capable of controlling fear. Morgan
and Thomson respect Random for his medical knowledge and
for his ability to win admiration and trust from his patients. He
is, in fact, shown as the best doctor aboard the ship—a bit of pride
excusable in the author, whose medical experiences, at least, must
have closely resembled those of his hero.

The midshipman, Crampley, is one of the least admirable characters in the novel. Brutal and malicious, he uses every means,
fair or foul, to make Random miserable. When his ship, in which
Roderick is surgeon, is wrecked off the French coast, Crampley,
then captain, is discovered to be not only inhuman but ignorant
of his profession as well. Midshipmen were generally disliked
because they frequently abused the authority they exercised over
the seamen. Masefield says that usually "they owed their appoint-
ments to interest."[54] Their duties consisted mostly of running
errands for the officer of the deck; though they were sometimes
entrusted with the command of small-boats, and with guard over
prisoners. They seem to have been poorly treated by their superiors and for the most part cordially detested by their inferiors.
Haulyard, midshipman in *The Reprisal,* is remarkable only for
his outspoken and domineering behavior aboard the French ship.

The chaplain of the *Thunder,* who is roughly handled by the

[54] Introduction to Walter, *A Voyage Round the World ... by George Anson,* p. 69.

author, is an arrant coward, as evidenced by his behavior in the cockpit during the bombardment, when he drinks with startling results:

The fumes of the liquor mounting into the parson's brain, conspired, with his former agitation of spirits, to make him quite delerious; he stript himself to the skin, and besmearing his body with blood, could scarce be withheld from running upon deck in that condition.[55]

Drunkenness among naval chaplains was common, and Flip, in Shadwell's play, says, "I am sure that our chaplains (generally speaking) are drunk as often as our sea-captains."[56] When Roderick is sick with fever, the chaplain urges him to auricular confession. Finding that the patient is a Presbyterian, however, he assures Random that nothing can be done, and returns to the convivial company in the wardroom.

Of the inferior, or warrant, officers in the navy, only Pipes, a boatswain, is clearly presented. Except that he is resourceful, honest, taciturn, and a good hand at a game, he is of little interest as a sailor. In the best navy manner he shrills his pipe, which is the only phase of his craft that he retains, and his aptitude for fighting accords with the temper of the other nautical figures in *Peregrine Pickle*.

It has been said that Smollett never showed the English sailor at his duties because, as surgeon's mate, he did not know enough actual seamanship to do so. Other critics suggest that the author did not want to clutter up his work with unnecessary details, as did Southey in *The Life of Nelson*. Be this as it may, little seamanship is to be found in the pages of *Roderick Random*. The reader is informed that the crew is divided into two watches, which work alternately, and that surgeon's muster is held every morning, but of little else.

One important character, Jack Rattlin, comes from the forecastle, however, and Rattlin's is one of the most sympathetic of

---

[55] Chap. 32.   [56] *The Fair Quaker of Deal* (1737), p. 47.

all Smollett's naval portraits. He is kind to Random on board the pressing tender, and later when he reappears with a broken leg he makes no complaint of the pain, his chief concern being to keep Mackshane from amputating it. At Boca Chica, although his hand is smashed, he knocks down the frenzied chaplain and otherwise shows the greatest intrepidity. The fact that he loses the hand seems to indicate that the author, who took a paternal interest in his sympathetic characters, felt that the sailor would be better off ashore minus one hand than to continue in the service. Rattlin is, throughout the reader's acquaintance with him, a real English seaman, one of the few to be found in literature. The type is generally considered to be extinct since steel and steam have taken the place of wood and canvas.

Ben Block, in *The Reprisal,* is the other seaman to be considered. His character is exaggerated, of course, for comic dramatic effect. His rifling of the personal effects aboard a captured ship is typical, it seems, of the seaman at the time, who felt, as Block explains it, that "all's fair plunder between decks." If he seems ridiculous when he dresses in stolen finery, the reader should bear in mind the conduct of Lieutenant Brett's party at the taking of Paita, on Anson's voyage:

> ...the sailors...could not be prevented from entering the houses which lay near them...where the first thing that occurred to them being the cloathes that the Spanish in their flight had left behind them ...our people eagerly seized these glittering habits and put them on over their own dirty trouzers and jackets, not forgetting, at the same time, the tye or bag-wig and laced hat...but those who came latest into the fashion, not finding men's cloaths sufficient to equip themselves, were obliged to take up with women's gowns and petticoats, which (provided there was finery enough) they made no scruples of putting on and blending with their own greasy dress.[57]

Block's drunken insubordination doubtless found many parallels in an age when navy crews consisted of the lowest dregs of society,

---

[57] Walter, *op. cit.,* p. 182.

in a calling where drunkenness is still, two hundred years later, the accepted reward for hardship and danger.

The unruliness of sailors at the capture of an enemy's ship or city is like that displayed when the *Lizard,* in *Roderick Random,* is wrecked, and the crew, "according to custom, broke up the chests belonging to the officers, dressed themselves in their clothes, drank their liquors without ceremony."[58] In similar circumstances, when H.M.S. *Wager* struck a sunken rock,

... numbers of them [i.e., the crew], instead of consulting their safety ... fell to pillaging the ship, arming themselves with the first weapons that came to hand and threatening to murder all who should oppose them. This frenzy was greatly heightened by the liquor they found on board, with which they got ... extremely drunk ... the men conceived that, by the loss of the ship, the authority of the officers was at an end.[59]

The same ship is wrecked in Bulkeley and Cummins' *A Voyage to the South Seas,*[60] the incident which Mr. Watson thinks Smollett used for the *Random* shipwreck;[61] and we are told:

They [some of the sailors] began with broaching the wine in the Lazaretto; then breaking open Cabins and Chests, arming themselves with Swords and Pistols, threatening to murder those who should oppose or question them; Being drunk and mad with Liquor, they plunder'd Chests and Cabins for Money and other Things of Value, cloathed themselves in the richest apparel they could find, and imagined themselves, Lords Paramount.

Withal, the navy man as pictured by Smollett is, as a rule, brave and pugnacious, faithful and honest. The lack of courage shown by the French in *The Reprisal,* and the parsimonious behavior of Bowling's Dutch companions in France, are evidences of that pride in the English sailor which, at the end of the century, was to bring forth plays in great number, all with the glorification of

---

[58] Chap. 57.
[59] Walter, *op. cit.,* pp. 139–140.
[60] (London, 1743), pp. 12–13.
[61] Watson, *The Sailor in English Fiction and Drama, 1550–1800* (New York, 1930), pp. 166–168.

the British seaman as their theme. In the mid-century, however, as Mr. Fletcher says,

Tipsy Jack, flinging his money away royally ... was always a favorite; but sober, hardworking Jack at sea, or broken-down Jack, maimed and useless, money, health, and merriment gone, interested nobody. Of the qualities that made the sailor what he was the country knew little and apparently cared less.[62]

CONCLUSION

The British navy was much as Smollett pictured it. Critics agree that this is true, although their reactions to his characters have been less consistent. Contemporary authorities, as well as modern scholars, bear witness that the abuses pictured in *Roderick Random* and in the *Account* did exist, that bribery and favoritism were common, that brutality and ignorance were not unknown. Namier speaks of the navy as being, by its very nature, a democratic service; but the reader who studies Namier's own work will find that he actually proves it to have been undemocratic, in every sense of the word, at this period. Naval historians have glossed the details and ignored the facts to no avail; the picture is drab at best, at worst it is horrible.

Yet from this background came such characters as Bowling and Trunnion, Thomson and Tomlins, precursors of the "hearts of oak" to be featured in novel and drama fifty years later. The naval novel, beginning with Smollett, continued in the work of writers like Chamier, and reached consummation a century later at the hands of Frederick Marryatt. During the interim much had happened: reforms under Anson and Nelson; the victories of the Nile, the Baltic, and Trafalgar; the introduction into general use of the frigate, lighter and faster than the old ships of the line; the adoption of retirement and pension, bringing younger men ahead; the improvement of sanitary practices; and the adoption of standard uniforms.

---

[62] "The Traditional British Sailor," *Nineteenth Century*, XLVIII (Sept., 1900), 434.

Smollett has been credited with the impetus for some of this reform, although he was rather a satirist than an avowed reformer. It may be, however, that the realistic picture and bitter comments with which he presented his naval experiences at Cartagena had some effect on later legislators. The frequency with which serious historians, from his own time to the present, have drawn from his work, testifies to the accuracy of his observation. Naval men have been less kind to his abilities as critic of his superiors in the service, and to his reflections on tactical matters; yet even they have quoted him as an authority. Whether or not he is reliable as a judge of the technical side of naval warfare is of little interest to the student of literature, except as a phenomenon independent of his abilities as creative artist. For the purpose of the present paper, which is concerned rather with factual detail than with philosophical reflection, it may be said that Smollett is dependable as no author not personally acquainted with the naval scene could have been in work of this kind.

In his handling of naval characters, he is superior to both predecessors and immediate followers. That the English sailor was not new to English literature when *Roderick Random* appeared, is evident to the most casual reader. Beowulf, although not a sailor, was a sea rover; Chaucer's Shipman bears the indelible stamp of his profession; Shakespeare's plays contain many seamen. The British navy had hostages in the literary camp in the persons of such characters as Flip and Manly. Yet with Smollett a relatively new factor enters the field—the personal acquaintance of the artist with actual life at sea.

Most of his characters are caricatures, even when sympathetically treated. In *Roderick Random,* for example, only the hero is presented as a natural man, and that only when he is in the navy. It has been shown how the author makes Tom Bowling, for example, stand out among his surroundings. This arresting quality enables the novelist to use broad, bright strokes in his portraits without creating in the reader a sense of undue incongruity. The same tendency to accentuate peculiarities is apparent in the work of Hogarth, especially in "Marriage à la Mode" and the two "Progresses"; and Smollett's gun-deck scenes are close kin to "Gin Lane." Smollett's intention in most of his work was satirical. To some extent this detracts from his value as a realist, because it frequently leads the author to overemphasize inconsequential details. The most important thing to be remembered by the modern student, however, is that "realism" is not only a modern term, but represents a distinction neither considered by the creative artist nor accepted by the critic in the eighteenth century. The standard by which Smollett is judged here is of our creation, not of his. The method which he used in his work relating to the sea, while it left something to be desired from the standpoint of modern realism, was the closest approach to a realistic treatment of such material that had appeared in literature up to that time.

The brutality of Oakum, the effeminacy of Whiffle, were not unknown in the navy in the first half of the eighteenth century. Nor, we may be sure, were "originals" like Morgan and Bowling, Ben Block, Occleber, and McClaymore. In that period regional differences between the denizens of different parts of the British Isles were more pronounced than they are today. Further, at a time when sea voyages were of long duration, when navy seamen were confined on shipboard even in English ports, individual peculiarities were accentuated more than they would have been ashore at that time, or are today even at sea. These facts must continually be kept in mind by the modern reader, to whom the characters treated are so different from anyone with whom his experience has familiarized him that they seem grossly exaggerated.

To the period also belongs much of the cold casualness with which Smollett treats moral corruption. His penchant for loathsome details, especially as regards the necessary acts of metabolism, indicates that he possessed, in extraordinary degree, the strong stomach and the disregard for niceties of human privacy, so necessary to the physician of his time.

Smollett's philosophy, as shown through the medium of his seafaring characters, seems to sum itself up in the picture of life as a fighting, hating, wanting time, and death as the last act of a Rabelaisian comedy. He never approaches religion except so far as he feels that, after all, death cannot be much worse than this life. This gives him a flippancy of attitude toward the troubles of this world that is closely related to the scorn evinced by philosophers and early church writers alike.

SMOLLETT AND THE "CRITICAL REVIEW"

II. SMOLLETT AND THE "CRITICAL REVIEW"

DRIVEN throughout his life by need of money,[1] although he seems to have earned enough to have kept a provident man in comfort, Smollett turned to publisher's jobs of all kinds. One phase of his many-sided activities was the editorship, from 1756 to about 1762, of the *Critical Review,* which during his lifetime employed the pens of such writers as Samuel Johnson, David Hume, Oliver Goldsmith, and William Robertson.

Despite the interest which students of literature from Scott to Henley have evinced in Smollett, and the many collected editions of his works which have appeared, no one has made a detailed study of his labors as a reviewer. Nor have his known essays been collected, as have those of Goldsmith and Johnson. But many of the quarrels which studded his literary career originated in his work as a critic, and it is from these quarrels and from Smollett's correspondence that most of our information concerning the early days of the *Critical* is derived.

It is interesting, in view of the later hostilities between the *Critical* and the *Monthly,* that Smollett's critical training was gained, in part at least, under the direction of Ralph Griffiths, editor of the *Monthly Review.*[2] Griffiths was himself a writer and, during his half century as editor, contributed many articles to the *Monthly.*[3] He was accused by his contemporaries, including writers for the *Critical,* of employing his wife, who died in 1764,

---

[1] In *Letters,* see pp. 8, 9, 24, 25, 37, 38, 41, 43, 49, 64, 74, 75, 78, 79. This is also apparent in the hitherto unnoticed MS ("Ts. S'tt.") which appeared at the Joline sale in 1913 (see item 499, Cat. IV, from which this description is taken). This MS, dated from "Chelsea, Wednesday Evening," says in part: "I was in hopes of hearing from you before this time, my affairs are very pressing."

[2] This, the first real review in a modern sense, was established in 1749. Griffiths, a Presbyterian ex-watchmaker, had begun his career as publisher under the guidance of Jacob Robinson, with whom he entered partnership in 1740.

[3] See Benjamin Christie Nangle, *The Monthly Review, First Series, 1749–1789. Indexes of Contributors and Articles* (Oxford, 1934). This work is based on a marked set of the *Monthly,* and my ascriptions of authorship in that periodical follow Mr. Nangle's study.

to revise contributions, although he denied this: "I can with the most sacred truth declare that there never was a single word written for the Review by a female pen, unless it were a few lines by the learned Miss C[arter] of D[eal]."⁴ Griffiths devoted all his time to the *Monthly,* assumed sole responsibility for its contents, assigned books for criticism, and read all copy. This centralization of control in the hands of a man who made editorship his main means of livelihood seems to have been unique until the nineteenth-century reviews made it an editorial policy. The *Critical* was to borrow from the *Monthly* a policy of anonymity, the practice of publishing each month's issue at the beginning of the following month, the inclusion of a "Monthly Catalogue" for brief mentions, and the use of extensive quotation in long reviews.

Smollett, by 1751, when his first contribution appeared in the *Monthly,* had already established himself as the author of a popular novel and as a translator. In 1748, *Roderick Random* had appeared and been accredited to Fielding, much to the real author's disgust no doubt. In the following year, Smollett's translation of *Gil Blas* was published, and in 1750⁵ second editions of both were issued. Hence he was no tyro when, in the October number of the *Monthly,* he enthusiastically reviewed John Cleland's *Memoirs of a Coxcomb.*⁶ Smollett's next contribution to this review concerned William Smellie's *Theory and Practice of*

⁴ (Quoted in *DNB* article, "Griffiths, Ralph.") This Miss Carter may be the "C——R, C, C–r" whom Nangle (p. 12) thinks to be Thomas Comber, and who contributed fifteen articles reviewing agricultural books between February, 1771, and July, 1773.

⁵ The mid-century year was eventful for Smollett, who obtained his medical doctorate from Marischal College, Aberdeen, in June. Soon afterwards he left for Paris and on his return settled in Chelsea, where he was to remain until 1763 (see Lewis Knapp, "Smollett's Early Years in London," *JEGPh,* XXXI [April, 1932], 220–227). In September, 1750, he complains (*Letters,* p. 10) to Dr. John Moore, his earliest biographer and the author of *Zeluco,* of the "fatigue of my present employment." This may refer to *Peregrine Pickle,* which was published in February, 1751.

⁶ The review appears in V (Oct., 1751), 52–56. Smollett's acquaintance with Cleland may have begun with the latter's favorable notice in the *Monthly* (I [May, 1749], 72–79) of Smollett's tragedy, *The Regicide,* which is spoken of as "one of the best theatrical pieces that has appeared these many years." The same reviewer wrote the criticism of *Peregrine Pickle* (IV [April, 1751], 355–358).

Midwifery,[7] and is especially interesting because he himself had edited Smellie's treatise. Just why Smollett did not continue to contribute to the *Monthly* after his review of John Pringle's *Observations on the Diseases of the Army* in July, 1752,[8] is unknown. It may be, however, that his work for Griffiths was a financial stopgap, and that more important projects took all his time thereafter.

The next three years (1753–1755) were extremely busy ones for Smollett, and offer an impressive proof of his versatility. They also help to explain his worth in such an undertaking as the *Critical Review,* where width and diversity of knowledge and experience were necessary. During 1753, agreements for editorial work on a collection of Voyages,[9] on Smellie's second volume of *Midwifery,* and on Alexander Drummond's *Travels,*[10] indicate that Smollett's capacities were known and appreciated. *Ferdinand, Count Fathom,* which appeared at this time, brought the novelist additional fame as well as, perhaps, the enmity of some members of the legal profession.[11] In 1754, he translated a French work on economics[12] and prepared for the press Drummond's *Travels,*[13] a translation of *Don Quixote,*[14] and a "History of the

---

[7] V (Dec., 1751), 465–466. See, in this regard, my "Tobias Smollett on the 'Separation of the Pubic Joint in Pregnancy,' " *Medical Life,* XLI (June, 1934), 302–305. Smollett's agreement with the publishers for half the copyright of "Dr. Smellie's Second Volume of Midwifery" appears in *Letters,* p. 26.

[8] VII, pp. 52–56. Although Smollett was pressed for money during 1752 (see his begging note to Richard Oswald in *Letters,* pp. 11–13), he seems to have published little. At this time appeared *The Essay on the External Use of Water,* his longest contribution to medical literature; and a satire on Fielding, *Habbakuk Hilding,* which has been attributed to him on somewhat tenuous grounds.

[9] *Letters,* pp. 23–24.

[10] *Ibid.,* pp. 24–25.

[11] See Smollett's comments to Alexander Hume Campbell in *Letters,* pp. 21–23.

[12] *Journal Economique,* Paris, 1753. Smollett's translation, published in February, 1754, was called *Select Essays on Commerce, Agriculture, Mines, Fisheries, and other Useful Subjects.* This was unfavorably reviewed in the *Monthly,* X (March, 1754), 321, but received enthusiastic comment in *London Mag.,* XIII (Feb., 1754), 95; (March), 125–126; (May), 221–224; (July), 309–310.

[13] *Travels through different cities of Germany, Italy, Greece, and Several Parts of Asia as far as the Banks of the Euphrates, in a series of Letters.* For possible influences of this work on Smollett's own *Travels* see Noyes's comment in *Letters,* p. 134.

[14] For this Smollett was paid five years earlier (see *Letters,* p. 32).

German Empire,"[15] which probably became a section of *The Modern Part of the Universal History*[16] on which he worked for Samuel Richardson. In January of the following year Smollett's *Don Quixote* appeared and he made a trip to Scotland.

At this time he seems to have been concerned in an attempt to inaugurate an academy of letters, similar to that in France, and in launching a periodical in this connection. In 1759 Joseph Reed, dissatisfied with the *Critical's* treatment of his *Madrigal and Trulletta,* published *A Sop in the Pan for a Physical Critic* in which the following comment about Smollett appears:

> In the close of the year 1755 a certain Caledonian quack, by the courtesy of England called a Doctor of Physic, whose real or assumed name is Ferdinando Mac-Fathomless, formed a project for initiating the male inhabitants of this island in the use and management of the linguary weapon by the erection of a scolding amphitheatre. For this purpose, he selected and engaged on weekly salary about a dozen of the most eminent professors of Vociferation in this Academy; but, after he had been at a considerable expense, the unfortunate emperor could not get his project licensed.[17]

Whether or not Reed's information was correct is hard to determine, but in 1756 Smollett had written to Moore that the *Critical Review* "is a small branch of an extensive Plan which I last year projected for a sort of Academy of the belles Lettres; a Scheme which will one day I hope be put in Execution to its utmost extent."[18] Evidently this plan was unsuccessful, but it probably influenced Smollett's editorial procedure on the *Review,* which was launched under the aegis of Archibald Hamilton early in March of the year 1756.

Smollett's Work on the "Critical"

When Hamilton, the Edinburgh printer whose share in the Porteus riots had necessitated his leaving Scotland, founded the *Criti-*

---

[15] *Ibid.,* pp. 28–29.
[16] Published 1759–1766. See Smollett's statements in regard to this work in *Letters,* pp. 59, 65–68, 82.
[17] P. 4.   [18] *Letters,* p. 39.

cal, he had Smollett as associate.[1] Despite the policy of the *Critical* not to reveal the identity of its contributors, Smollett's connection with the periodical was well known, and he thus became the butt of many authors whose publications did not meet a favorable reception in the *Review.*[2]

As we have seen, Smollett had "broken in" on Griffith's *Monthly.* Another experience which helped him in editorial work was his employment of understrappers in the composition of his histories. Furthermore, he was a Scot and corresponded with many of his countrymen, from whom, as we shall see, he solicited contributions for the *Critical.* He was also a seasoned Grub Street campaigner and had taken part in several literary quarrels, experiences which stood him in good stead in his relations with disgruntled authors. All in all, he was one of the best men in London in 1756 for the work which he was to do for Hamilton's periodical.

The first number of the *Critical* appears for January and February, 1756. In the April issue the editors acknowledge[3] attacks made on the new review and mention an author who "declares war against a Scotch adventurer in wit and physic, who hacks at *random* the reputation of his betters." Obviously Smollett is meant by the "Scotch adventurer," showing that one angry author was already on his trail.

By July, 1756, Smollett's connection with the *Critical* was known to his friends in Scotland, for on August 3 he writes to Dr. Moore, "By your asking if I am engaged in any new performance, and immediately after mentioning the 'Critical Review' I conclude you have been told I am concerned in that work: your

---

[1] This connection may have begun at the printing establishment of William Strahan, for whom Hamilton had worked before starting out on his own. See L. M. Knapp, "Smollett's Works as Printed by William Strahan," *Library,* XIII (Dec., 1932), 282–291.

[2] During the period 1756–1771 the editors acknowledge seventy-eight such attacks, exclusive of articles in the newspapers (see Appendix B).

[3] I, 287–288. One should remember that the *Review* was published on or about the first of the following month, that is, the first (January–February) number probably appeared on the first of March.

information is true.'"[4] On August 10, 1756, he begins what is to prove a long series of apologies to acquaintances who blame him for unfavorable notices. He writes to Samuel Richardson as follows:

I was extremely concerned to find myself suspected of a Silly, mean Insinuation against Mr. Richardson's Writings, which appeared some time ago in the Critical Review[5] and I desired my friend Mr. Millar[6] to assure you in my name that it was inserted without my privity or concurrence.[7]

As a rule authors did not believe such apologies,[8] but there is no good reason to doubt the sincerity of Smollett's statement, because at this time he was engaged as editor of *The Modern Part of The Universal History,* a publication in which the author of *Clarissa* was also concerned.[9]

The only review during the first year which can be assigned to Smollett is the unfavorable notice of Rolt's *History of South America,* which appears in the March issue[10] and which includes one of the most convincing pictures we have of the mid-eighteenth-century Grub Street journeyman. Smollett's biographers have agreed in crediting him with the "Advertisements," or statements of purpose, which appear in the first volume, as well as with other articles in which they believe that his style is discern-

---

[4] *Letters,* p. 39.
[5] See I (April, 1756), 261: "Had the writer of *Sir Charles Grandison* been to have worked upon the materials of *The Supposed Daughter* [a novel], he would easily have swelled them into twenty folio volumes."
[6] Andrew Millar, the London printer and publisher.
[7] *Letters,* p. 40.
[8] Churchill's comments show how they were received by disgruntled authors:
> By int'rest join'd, th' expert confed'rates stand,
> And play the game into each others hand.
> The vile abuse, in turn by all deny'd,
> Is bandy'd up and down from side to side:
> It flies—hey!—presto!—like a jugler's ball,
> 'Till it belongs to nobody at all.
> ("The Apology," *Poems,* I [London, 1765], 61.)
[9] See Smollett's correspondence with Richardson in this connection in *Letters,* pp. 65, 66, 67–68.
[10] I, 97–106. Cf. *Letters,* p. 132.

ible.[11] Ascription is dubious, however, when based on the criterion of style or on such criteria as the use of indecent personalities and the frequency of Shakespeare quotations.

In 1757 Smollett disclaims authorship of the unfavorable review, which appeared in March,[12] of Home's *Douglas,* and tells his correspondent[13] that he "did not write one article in that whole number." Just what he did write for the *Review* during its second year we do not know, but on January 2 of the following year he tells Dr. Moore:

I have for some time done little in the *Critical Review:* the Remarks on Home's Tragedy[14] I never saw until they were in print and as yet I have not read one line of the Epigoniad. I am told that the work has merit and am truly sorry that it should have been so roughly handled.[15] Notwithstanding the censures that have been so freely bestowed upon these and other Productions of our Country, the authors of the *Critical Review* have been insulted and abused as a *Scotch Tribunal.* The Truth is, there is no author so wretched, but he will meet with countenance in England, if he attacks our nation in any shape. You cannot conceive the Jealousy that prevails against us.[16]

In May, 1758, Smollett's review of *The Conduct of Admiral Knowles on the Late Expedition Set in a True Light* appeared.[17]

---

[11] That such a criterion is not very satisfactory is obvious to anyone familiar with the two reviews where, as Churchill says of poetry,

> How doth it make judicious readers smile
> When authors are detected by their stile:
> Tho' ev'ry one who knows this author knows
> He shifts his stile much oftener than his cloaths?
> (*Op. cit.*, p. 62.)

This is true of Smollett, as can be seen by contrasting his *Essay on the External Use of Water,* his novels, his histories, and *The Adventures of an Atom.* Professional men of letters at this time had to be "all things to all men." See Lewis Benjamin, *The Life and Letters of Tobias Smollett (1721–1771),* by Lewis Melville [pseud.] (London, 1926), pp. 131–132, 137–139, 140; and George M. Kahrl, "The Influence of Shakespeare on Smollett," *Essays in Dramatic Literature,* ed. Hardin Craig (Princeton, 1935), pp. 394–420; Mr. Kahrl points out the dangers of ascribing authorship to Smollett on the basis of Shakespeare quotations.

[12] III, 258–268.

[13] Dr. John Moore; this appears in *Letters,* pp. 47–48.

[14] This was Home's *Douglas,* which was reviewed in the *Critical,* III (March, 1757), 258–268.

[15] In IV (July, 1757), 27–35; this review is attacked in David Hume's letter which was printed in the *Critical* on the appearance of the second edition of the poem: VII (Feb., 1759), 89–103.

[16] *Letters,* p. 51. [17] V, 438–439 (see Appendix A).

Smollett had already gone out of his way to hold the Admiral up to ridicule for his part in the unfortunate Cartagena campaign of 1740,[18] the details of which add so much vividness to his *Roderick Random*. This was, apparently, a heaven-sent opportunity to lash one of the notorious gentlemen-admirals of the time, and Smollett turned to it with a will. Among other details, he speaks of Knowles as "an admiral without conduct, . . . an officer without resolution, and a man without veracity" and "an ignorant, assuming, officious, fribbling pretender; conceited as a peacock, obstinate as a mule, and mischievous as a monkey."

Knowles, whatever his courage and judgment in line of duty, was not a forgiving man, and he had Hamilton, the publisher, arrested. Despite appeals to Wilkes[19] and others, Smollett could not cause enough pressure to be brought to bear on the Admiral to insure his withdrawal of the case; so Smollett gave himself up as the author of the offending article. He was fined one hundred pounds and sentenced to three months in the King's Bench Prison. The summary of the case which follows is taken from Blackstone:

The defendant was a nominal physician, in the bookseller's pay, and was convicted on an information for writing a libel against Admiral Knowles, in the Critical Review. He declared his sorrow for the offense, that he had offered the Admiral reasonable satisfaction, which was refused; and was now ready to do as the court should think proper. The Court (absente Foster J.) fined him 100 pounds, imprisoned him for three months, and ordered him to find security for good behaviour for seven years, himself in 500 pounds and two sureties 250 pounds each. And Lord Mansfield, C. J. added, that his submission had had its effect with the court.[20]

---

[18] In his account of the campaign in Dodsley's *Compendium of Voyages,* 1756 (reprinted in *Works*, XII, 187–221). See also *Roderick Random,* chaps. 24 to 34 inclusive. It is interesting to note that as late as 1907 Admiral Vernon, who commanded the Cartagena expedition, found an apologist, Douglas Ford, whose *Admiral Vernon and the Navy* (London) attacks Smollett.

[19] *Letters,* pp. 56, 58, 61, 62.

[20] *Report of Cases from 1746–1779* (London, 1828). Quoted in Whitridge, *Tobias Smollett,* p. 41 n.

Between the middle of October, 1759, and the end of February, 1760,[21] Smollett served his term in King's Bench Prison, where he was visited by his friends, including Garrick,[22] and where he seems to have written *Lancelot Greaves,* for his own newly established *British Magazine.*

The year 1759, during which Knowles was trying to discover the offending author, is one of the most important in the amount of information which survives, of those years during which Smollett was connected with the *Critical.* In the first place, two letters written at this time add considerably to our knowledge of his position on the *Review.* On March 15, Dr. William Robertson, author of the popular *History of Scotland,* writes to Smollett:

There was published a few weeks ago a book called "Historical Law Tracts." The author of it is Lord Kames, one of our judges, a man of great knowledge and worth, and the friend of every person in Scotland to whom you wish well. I intended (in consequence of a permission which you granted your Scotch friends in your last letter to Carlyle) to have drawn up an article for this book, to be inserted in the *Critical Review.* May I beg that you will either delay this book till next month, with some general compliment upon it, and that it shall then be considered at large; or if such a delay be now improper, let me entreat of you to look at the book, and the article prepared for it, yourself, and to see justice done to the merit of the performance, which I can assure you is very great.[23]

The phrase "in consequence of a permission which you granted your Scotch friends" indicates that some of the "Correspondent" reviews may have originated north of the Tweed.

---

[21] On Oct. 12, 1759, Smollett writes from Chelsea (see *Letters,* p. 68). On Feb. 21, 1760, William Huggins sends "Congratulations on my Dr. Friend's Restoration to his dear Liberty" (see L. F. Powell, "William Huggins and Tobias Smollett," *MP,* XXXIV [Nov., 1936], 188).

[22] See Smollett, *Letters,* p. 70. Benjamin claims (*op. cit.,* p. 180) that Wilkes and Goldsmith also went to see him, and this is very likely in view of the friendship between Smollett and Wilkes, and the connection between Smollett and Goldsmith on the *British Magazine* at this time. Smollett's description of the King's Bench Prison in *Lancelot Greaves* (chaps. 20 and 21) takes on added interest from his experience there, probably at the very time when he was composing it. He may also have contributed a short poem to the *British Magazine* at this time (see my note in *NQ,* CLXXIV, 152).

[23] Quoted by Benjamin, *op. cit.,* pp. 174–175. It is not known whether or not Robertson was the author of the review which appeared in the *Critical,* VIII (Nov., 1759), 391–394.

At any rate, Smollett's duties seem to have included the soliciting of outside contributions. This is probably the gist of a letter offered for sale[24] in 1935, and dated from Chelsea January 20, 1759. Smollett also writes to Dr. Macaulay in December, 1759, "I wish you could get me an article for the next number of the Review, on painting, statuary, or engraving."[25] It is possible that the few examples of the *Critical's* boasted account of painting and statuary, "in which they stand unrivalled by any periodical writer of this kingdom," were by Maucalay, or were solicited from others in this way.

During this year several disgruntled authors attacked the *Critical,* some of them through Smollett. Hence it is no wonder that he writes to Wilkes that he is "fain to snatch at a momentary respite from reading dull books and writing dull *Commentaries invita Minerva.*"[26] Probably he went abroad between April and October, 1759. On February 21, 1760, William Huggins, translator of Dante and Ariosto, congratulates Smollett on his enlargement from the King's Bench and invites him to Bath. Smollett replies, four days later, "were I not tied down to the stake by periodical publications, I would pay my respects to you in Somersetshire."[27] In April he writes to David Garrick:

I see Mr. Colman has taken offense at the article in the *Critical Review* which treats of the 'Rosciad,' and I understand he suspected me to be the author of the offensive article.... I shall leave him and the real author to settle the affair between themselves, and content myself with declaring to you, and that upon my honour, that I did not write one word of the article upon the 'Rosciad.' I must own, that if I had examined the article upon the 'Rosciad' before it was sent to the press, I should have put my negative upon some expressions in it...but I have been so hurried since my enlargement, that I had not time to write one article in the *Critical Review,* except that upon Bower's

---

[24] By James Tregaskis & Son, London. See their Catalogue No. 1019.

[25] *Letters,* p. 65. The quotation which follows is from the preface to the first volume of the *Critical,* 1756.

[26] *Letters,* p. 61. Concerning Smollett's trip abroad, see *ibid.,* p. 187.

[27] Quoted by L. F. Powell, *op. cit.,* p. 189. See also Huggins' invitation on p. 188. In another letter, written May 25, Smollett speaks of his "slavish engagements" (p. 190).

History, and perhaps I shall not write another these six months. That and a bad state of health, have prevented me from returning in person the visit you favoured me with in the King's Bench.[28]

This indicates that Smollett possessed the power to revise articles, a type of interference which the *Monthly* reviewers seem to have suffered. Garrick, it seems, was soon appeased, for in January, 1762, Smollett writes to him:

I this morning received your *Winter's Tale,* and am agreeably flattered by this mark of your attention. What I have said of Mr. Garrick in the *History of England,* was, I protest, the language of my heart.... Besides I thought it incumbent on me in particular to make a public atonement, in a work of truth, for wrongs done him in a work of fiction. Among other inconveniences arising from ill health, I deeply regret my being disabled from a personal cultivation of your goodwill, and from the unspeakable enjoyment I should sometimes derive from your private conversation.[29]

The play referred to is *Florizel and Perdita* (Garrick's alteration of Shakespeare's *The Winter's Tale*), which received considerable praise in the February number of the *Critical,*[30] possibly at Smollett's hands. The history mentioned is the Continuation of the *History of England,* which contains, in a section devoted to the state of the "republic of letters" in the reign of George II, panegyrics on several men whom Smollett had attacked earlier, including Fielding, Akenside, and Lyttleton.

During part of 1762, Smollett traveled for his health, as he had in 1761,[31] but on August 19 he writes to Moore:

Your conjecture is right in supposing that I still write for the *Critical Review.* As I am proprietor of that work I should be a fool to give

[28] *Letters,* pp. 69–70. The *Rosciad* article referred to occurs in XI (March, 1761), 209–212. The article on Archibald Bower's *History of the Popes* appeared in the same number, pp. 185–193.
[29] *Letters,* p. 72. In the *Continuation* (IV, 126) Smollett had said:
"The exhibitions of the stage were improved to the most exquisite entertainment by the talents and management of Garrick, who greatly surpassed all his predecessors of this, and perhaps every other nation, in his genius for acting, in the sweetness and variety of his tones, the irresistible magick of his eye, the fire and vivacity of his action, the elegance of attitude, and the whole pathos of expression."
[30] XIII, 157–158.   [31] See Powell, *op. cit.,* p. 191.

it up at a time when it begins to indemnify me for all the vexation and loss I have sustained by it; but the laborious part of authorship I have long resigned. My constitution will no longer allow me to toil as formerly.[32]

Probably most of the "vexation and loss" was occasioned by the Knowles affair. It is difficult to understand why, if he was a member of a syndicate and chief editor, Smollett was just beginning to be indemnified for his work on the *Critical,* since that journal seems to have been extremely popular. Writing to an American correspondent early in the following year, Smollett includes in a "genuine list" of his productions a "great part of the Critical Review."[33] If this is to be taken literally, it means that for the first five or six years of the journal's existence he must have been a major contributor.

On November 4, 1762, however, Boswell makes the following entry in his journal:

Smollett . . . writes now very little in the *Critical Review.* Mr. Francklin, Greek professor at Cambridge, and Mr. Campbell, Son to a Principal Campbell of St. Andrews, write in it. It is an invidious task. Every month there are about 70 authors and during the year not above 2 good ones.[34]

In June, 1763, Smollett goes abroad for his health, on the trip he is to describe in his *Travels in France and Italy,* and remains away from England for two years, until July, 1765. In April of that year, the editors, possibly with him in mind, although he hardly seems an ideal reviewer of theological works, inform Mr. Bulkley that "the gentleman, to whose province it [i.e., Bulkley's *Œconomy of the Gospels*] more immediately belongs, has for some time been absent upon a journey."[35] In November, 1765, Smollett writes as follows.

---

[32] E. S. Noyes, "Another Smollett Letter," *MLN,* XLII (April, 1927), 232.
[33] *Letters,* p. 81.
[34] Malahide papers, I, 137. This may suggest Campbell as Smollett's successor, an office which Dr. Francklin, absent from London, would have found almost impossible.
[35] XX (April, 1765), 167–168.

I gave up all concern in the *Critical Review,* and every other literary system before I quitted England. Since my return I have written a few articles merely for amusement; but I have now no concern in that work.[36]

In December, 1766, the editors speak of his connection with the *Critical* as follows:

... Dr. Smollett (who bye the bye, has not, for several years past, had the least concern with the *Critical Review*).... We have thought to apprize our readers of this circumstance as we have lately seen the Doctor abused in several publications, on the supposition of his being still concerned in this *Review*.[37]

Some of the authors, however, refused to credit this assertion, as appears by the dedication to George Canning's *An Appeal to the Publick, from the Malicious Misrepresentations of the Critical Reviewers,* which appeared in 1767:

To Tobias Smollett, M.D. Uniformly tenacious of the Principles he was nursed in—famous for His stories, Histories, and His continued Continuations of His Complete Histories, as the Single Personage with whom the unnamed putters-together of the Critical Review Utterly disclaim all manner of connection (Graceless Rogues!—Disown their Father!) the ensuing Tractate is with singular propriety most cordially inscribed by its Author.[38]

In February, 1767, Smollett writes from Bath, where he had gone to recuperate from a serious illness:

I am almost stupefied with ill health, Loss of Memory, Confinement and Solitude; and I believe in my Conscience, the Circulation would have stopped of itself, if it was not every now and then stimulated by the stings of my Grub Street Friends, who attack me in the public Papers. Some times I am baited as a dunce then a ministerial Hireling, then a Jacobite, then a rancorous Knave, then a Liar, Quack and assassin.

In 1768 the *Critical* editors are still trying to convince the public of Smollett's nonparticipation in the *Review*.

---

[36] *Letters,* p. 96.
[37] XXXII, 434 and n.
[38] Quoted by Noyes in *Letters,* p. 216. Smollett's comments, which follow, occur in *Letters,* p. 102. The authors of the newspaper attacks during this period have not, so far as I know, been identified.

...that Dr. Smollett has within these few years written part of the *Critical Review* ... is a notorious untruth (as may be proved upon oath in a court of justice).[39]

In the following year, he left England for Italy, where he died in 1771. Four years after his death appeared what may be a reference to one of his early reviews. The writer says, as to certain mistakes which appeared in the *Critical*'s estimate of Gray's *Ode on the Progress of Poetry,* in 1757:

But the author of that article has not been concerned in this review for twelve years past and probably he may now be gone to that place, where it is not in his power to 'fall into a ridiculous blunder,' 'to chew on Greek quotations' or to speak for himself.[40]

Whoever were his successors on the *Critical* after he left for the Continent in 1763, Smollett undoubtedly was responsible, through his own work and the work of those whose contributions he enlisted during the *Critical*'s first eight years, for the *Review*'s popularity. Certainly an editor who succeeded in obtaining the services of such literary men as Goldsmith and Johnson, such historians as Hume and Robertson, such a scholar as Francklin, and such a doctor as Hunter, deserves a measure of credit. The articles which these men wrote differ considerably from those which we find in literary reviews today, but the essays in the *Critical* attained a degree of popularity denied to most of our own reviews; and much, if not most, of this popularity came to the *Review* through the efforts of Tobias George Smollett.

"Critical" Opponents and Contributors

As we have seen, Smollett's connection with the *Critical* resulted in several exchanges of unpleasantness with dissatisfied authors and rival publications. The most constant opponent of Hamilton's journal was *The Monthly Review*. In addition to this periodical, which employed a considerable battery of talent, three individual attackers managed to pierce the *Critical*'s armor during Smol-

---

[39] XXV (April, 1768), 277.   [40] XXXIV (June, 1775), 462 n.

lett's reign. They were, in order of appearance in the arena: Thomas Shebbeare, James Grainger, and Charles Churchill.

In 1757 Thomas Shebbeare, party journalist and miscellaneous writer extraordinary, published his *The Occasional Critic, or the Decrees of the Scotch Tribunal in the Critical Rejudged,* in which he excoriated Smollett as head of the journal. The *Critical* answered in kind,[1] and Shebbeare returned to the attack with his *Appendix to the Occasional Critic* in which he averred that the *Critical* was prejudiced in favor of Scotch authors, and that Smollett would "undertake to praise all works be they never so bad . . . in the *Critical Review,* for very small gratuities."[2] Shebbeare's assertion that, for a financial consideration, the editors would praise any book is common in attacks on the *Critical;* the most conclusive of all denials by the *Review* is as follows:

We hereby offer a reward of 50 guineas, to be paid by the printer of this work, to any person who shall prove that the *Critical Review* was ever under the direction or influence of any bookseller whatsoever, or that any person concerned in the Review from its first institution, ever received any present or bribe, or other unfair consideration, for any article that ever it contained;—we say *unfair* consideration, because some of the Reviewers have been honestly paid by the proprietors for their labour; and a few books, at their first publication, have been sent as presents to one or other of the supposed proprietors of the work.[3]

Shebbeare's designation of the *Critical* as a "Scotch Tribunal" also struck fire from the editors, who, in October, 1757, say[4] that "of five persons engaged in writing the Critical Review, only one is a native of Scotland." This *one* is evidently Smollett, whose connection with the *Critical* was so definitely established as common knowledge that the reviewer of his *History* felt free to mention Smollett as "colleague."[5]

[1] IV (April, 1757), 332.
[2] As quoted by Arnold Whitridge, *Tobias Smollett,* p. 30.
[3] XV (Jan., 1763), 82.
[4] IV, 333.
[5] III (June, 1757), 481.

Whether or not any Scots besides Smollett were connected with the *Review* in an editorial capacity is unknown, although Hamilton, whose name appeared on the title page after the fourth volume, was obviously a Scot; and there may well have been contributors from Scotland at this time, as there were two years later. Authors continued, however, to consider, or say that they considered, the *Critical* a Scotch organ, as is shown by the Scotticisms in *The Battle of the Reviews'* catalogue of authors connected with the journal, and by Churchill's lines:

> Tho Scot with Scot, in damned close intrigues
> Against the Commonwealth of letters leagues.[6]

The second of these authors to attack the *Critical* through Smollett was James Grainger, who was associated with Griffiths on the *Monthly,* and whose translation of Tibullus' *Elegies* had been unfavorably noticed by Smollett in the rival publication.[7] His *A Letter to Tobias Smollett, M.D. Occasioned by his Criticism upon a Translation of Tibullus,* in 1758, brought forth an answer from the *Critical,* which contained the following:

... whenever we think that the employment of writing for subsistence requires an apology, we shall know how to excuse it ... the dishonor does not lie in writing, but in writing without genius. Dr. Smollett has been a professed author from his early youth and generally succeeded in many different kinds of writing ... his works are at this day bought up with avidity, and read with applause by half the nation ... while Grainger is an obscure hireling, in the *Monthly Review,* under the inspection and correction of an illiterate bookseller.... That Dr. Smollett does keep house, and lives like a gentleman, divers authors of this age can testify, and among the rest, Dr. James Grainger. ... It is not true that authors have been solicited to hand characters of their own work to the *Critical Review,* which not a few have complied with.... The *Critical Review* is not written by a parcel of obscure hirelings, under the restraint of a bookseller, and his wife, who pre-

---

[6] "The Apology," *Poems,* I, 61.

[7] *Critical,* IV (Dec., 1758), 475–482. Grainger was told by his publisher, Millar, that Smollett had "been at" the translation. See Grainger's letter quoted by Benjamin, *The Life and Letters of Tobias Smollett,* pp. 135–136.

sume to revise, alter, and amend the articles occasionally. The principal writers in the *Critical Review* are unconnected with booksellers, unawed by old women, and independent of each other.[8]

However the article may err on the side of harshness with respect to Grainger and Griffiths, the reviewer certainly deserves praise for his refusal to be awed by the customary "gentleman author" attitude.

In 1761 the reviewer of the *Rosciad,* claiming to recognize the style of George Colman and Robert Lloyd in the poem, attacked the work as an unfair jibe at several competent actors. The letters of Lloyd and Colman in the public papers,[9] in which they denied any part in the poem, are unimportant; but Charles Churchill, the real author, swung into action the heaviest onslaught which had been aimed at the *Review* up to this time.

In his *An Apology Addressed to the Critical Reviewers,* which is chiefly directed at Smollett, Churchill exposes the novelist and his fellow critics to public ridicule with a dexterity which, even today, provokes laughter. This mock apology, a favorite form of derision, considers the anonymity of the critics, their boasted ability to detect authors by style, their candor, and their freedom from outside influence. Other abuse the *Critical* was destined to receive, yet the future did not bring forth any one criticism, solemn or humorous, to compare with this. Nor did Churchill forget his opponents, as appears in *The Ghost* (1762–1763), the *Epistle to William Hogarth* (1763), *The Candidate* (1764), and *Gotham* (1764).

The editors of the *Critical* acknowledged such attacks in the following terms.

[8] VII (Feb., 1759), 147–151. The review appears on pp. 141–158. This may have been written by Goldsmith, who is said by Isaac Reed to have written a "Defence of Dr. Smollett against Dr. Grainger" in 1759. See Katherine C. Balderston, *A Census of the Manuscripts of Oliver Goldsmith* (New York, 1926), pp. 38–39, 51–52.

[9] Referred to in the *Critical* article on Churchill's *Apology,* XXVII (June, 1771), 409. Eugene R. Page, in his *George Colman the Elder* (New York, 1935), pp. 64–67, presents the "triumvirate" side of the case, which he upholds with considerable zeal.

One gentleman, in particular, whose character stands in some degree of favour with the public, has been singled out as a victim, and galled by all the shafts of malignity. He has not only felt the rod of persecution and prosecution for opinions which he really broached, but he has been insulted in public abuse, and traduced in private calumny, by obscure authors whom he did not know, for criticisms he had not written on performances he never saw.[10]

Interesting as are these attacks and counterattacks, it is even more important to consider the authors conjectured to have contributed to the *Critical* or known to have contributed to it. In the first place, the question of identities of editors other than Smollett presents itself. Writing in August, 1756, the author of *Roderick Random* says that "the 'Critical Review' is conducted by four gentlemen of approved abilities, and meets with a very favourable reception."[11] Who the other three were, if Smollett included himself, is not known. The editor of the *Letters* conjectures that they may have been Dr. Thomas Francklin, David Mallock (or Mallett), and Griffith Jones.[12] Courtney, in the *DNB* article on Francklin, says that he "was one of the contributors to the *Critical Review*" and that "one of his victims was Arthur Murphy"; there is no proof, however, that this versatile Cambridge professor of Greek was connected with the *Review* in any other capacity.[13] Mallock is also supposed to have contributed to the *Critical*,[14] but there is no indication that Griffith Jones was concerned in it except the very fragile connection afforded by his association with Goldsmith and Smollett in the *British Magazine* six years later.

If Smollett meant four editors besides himself, Noyes suggests Joseph Robertson, who does not appear, however, to have begun contributing to the journal until eight years afterward. The

---

[10] XI (Preface, 1761), 1.

[11] *Letters*, p. 39.

[12] See *Letters*, pp. 148–149.

[13] Boswell mentions him as a *Critical* reviewer in November, 1762. (See Malahide papers, I, 127.)

[14] Boswell, *Life of Johnson,* ed. Hill, II, 409 n.

anonymous author of Robertson's obituary in the *Gentleman's Magazine* for February, 1802, says that Robertson wrote 2,620 articles for the *Critical* between August, 1769, and September, 1785. This evidence is further strengthened by the statement "I have Mr. Robertson's sett of the *Critical Review,* in which he has particularly marked his own articles."[15] Although this set, like the one marked by Thomas Wright according to Hamilton's directions, has disappeared,[16] there seems to be no good reason to connect Robertson with the journal before 1764.

Further, just who took Smollett's place on the *Critical* when he left for the Continent in 1763 is difficult to determine. Possibly it was William Guthrie, whom Nichols calls editor,[17] and to whom Percival Stockdale refers as a "chief contributor" in 1770. Stockdale, who took Guthrie's place when the latter died in that year, wrote the following account, which is the most authentic we have after Smollett left the *Review:*

Early in the spring of 1770, Dr. GUTHRIE died;—he was a Scotch gentleman of good abilities; and he had acquired some distinction as an author; he was one of those ill-fated men, who without fortune, and without powerful and effectual friends, depend greatly, for their subsistence, on employment from booksellers. He had written in the critical review; of which, at that time, the redoubted chieftan, was Mr. HAMILTON; a prosperous and very affluent printer, who lived in falconcourt, in fleet street. This man called on me, one morning, at my lodgings in holborne;—he acquainted me with the news of GUTHRIE's death; and offered me the succession to his province in the critical review; which was that of polite literature. I did not like the offer; but money was indispensably necessary. The payment to the writers in that review was poor; viz: two guineas a sheet:—however, as it was very convenient for me to give some regard to the proposal, I insisted on very manly, and spirited conditions, for one in my circumstances:—I told Mr. HAMILTON, that I was willing to enter into the literary department of his review, of which he was so civil as to give me the first offer; provided I should not be obliged to review such books as I did not like to review; and that I should give

---

[15] LXXII, p. 110. Robertson may have succeeded Stockdale, in 1771.
[16] Nichols, *Illustrations,* II, 399.
[17] *Literary Anecdotes,* III, 48 n.

my free, unobstructed, and in every way, unaltered sentiments on those that I did review. He acquiesced in my terms; and in march, 1770, I first appeared, but under the cover of the master of the seven-fold shield; as an arbiter of the fate of authors.—I proceeded in my censorial office till April of the next year; when I proposed to our general, an augmentation of my pay. The boldest dashers of the monthly reviewers, for their unmerited, and capricious protection; and for their dark and inhuman assassinations, were requited by GRIFFITHS, the khan of that horde, with four guineas a sheet. My grand signor met my demand with a positive refusal. My narrow purse was a little more contracted by this rupture; but my heart was enlarged, and played more vigorously.[18]

Whoever were the editors during Smollett's lifetime, they succeeded in engaging as authors three of their greatest contemporaries: Oliver Goldsmith, Samuel Johnson, and David Hume. The historian's connection with the *Review* seems to have been slight, but Goldsmith and Johnson were more concerned in it.

During the second year of its existence, the *Critical* contains one article[19] by Oliver Goldsmith, who was to contribute much to its later fame. In May, 1750, Smollett writes to Dr. Moore:

The little Irishman, about whom you express some curiosity, was my amanuensis, and has been occasionally employed as a Trash reader for the Critical Review, but you are not to number him among my companions nor indeed does his character deserve any further Discussion.[20]

Since Smollett was concerned, at this time, in several works requiring considerable "hackney writing"[21] his need for an amanuensis was probably great. It would be interesting to know whether Goldsmith, who was small, had been so employed on the *Critical* before he worked on the *Monthly*. If so, the story of Smollett's

---

[18] *The Memoirs of Percival Stockdale* (London, 1809), II, 57–58.

[19] Review of Ovid's *Fasti,* tr. William Massey, in IV (Nov., 1757), 402–404.

[20] *Letters,* p. 46.

[21] His *Compendium of Voyages* in 7 volumes was published by Dodsley in 1756, and the *Complete History of England,* in 4 volumes, appeared in the following year. It may be that actual work on the latter furnished Goldsmith with the basis for his own *History of England,* which was compiled from Smollett, Hume, and others. And see *Letters,* p. 161. For the publication of Smollett's histories, see Lewis M. Knapp, "The Publication of Smollett's 'Complete History and Continuation,'" *Library,* XVI (Dec., 1935), 295–301.

rescuing him from the Griffiths household, much as medieval damsels were rescued from ogres, needs salting.

Bishop Percy thus describes the conditions under which Goldsmith had been living with the Griffiths family:

In this thraldom he lived for 7 or 8 months, Griffiths and his wife continually objecting to everything he wrote and insisting on his implicitly submitting to their corrections and since Dr. Goldsmith lived with Griffiths and his wife during this intercource the Dr. and he thought it incumbt. to drudge for his Pay constantly from 9 o'clock till 2. The above agreement [to write for the *Monthly* "in consideration of his board, Lodging, and 100 *Pd. per annum"*] (which was in writing) was to hold for a twelve-month.[22]

It has been thought that the comments on hack writing and review criticism which appear in Goldsmith's *An Enquiry into the Present State of Polite Learning*[23] were inspired by his apprenticeship under Griffiths, but there is no reason to suppose that he had the *Monthly* in mind any more than the *Critical,* and both journals expressed their disapproval.[24] However this may be, he seems to have been known as a writer on the *Critical* in 1760 to the author of *The Battle of the Reviews,* who apparently means to designate Goldsmith by the "Paddy Fitzpatrick" whom he lists as understrapper to "Sampson MacJackson" and "Sawney MacSmallhead."[25] The bulk of Goldsmith's articles, as listed by Gibbs,[26] appear in the *Critical* from January to September, 1759.

[22] Katherine C. Balderston, *The History and Sources of Percy's Memoir of Goldsmith* (Cambridge [Eng.], 1926), p. 16. Miss Balderston points out (p. 32 n.) that the MS version used here was toned down before its inclusion in the edition of Goldsmith's works which appeared under the auspices of the principal London publishers in 1801.

[23] Chaps. x–xi. The *Enquiry* was published in 1759.

[24] The *Critical* comment appears in VII (April, 1759), 369–372. William Kendrick was the author of the article in the *Monthly,* XXI (Oct., 1759), 381.

[25] This nickname for Smollett seems to have originated with Dr. John Hill, and the *Critical* advises a hostile author, who has been facetious about Smollett's first name, to consult Hill, who has called Smollett "Smallhead" (VII [Feb., 1759], 143). Noyes quotes the *Battle* in part, pp. 149–150.

[26] Ed. *Works of Oliver Goldsmith,* I (London, 1884), 409–412. The reviews are reprinted by Gibbs on pp. 300–303, 322–406. For further details, see *New Essays by Oliver Goldsmith,* ed. Ronald S. Crane (Chicago, 1927), pp. xii, xiv, xv, xxvi. Information concerning Goldsmith's contributions to *The British Magazine,* and reprints of them, are on pp. vii, xii, xiv, xvi, xviii, xxxvi, 1–11, 112, 133–136.

Since he apparently contributed a considerable part of *The British Magazine* which he and Smollett started in the following year, Goldsmith probably had little time for the *Critical* after 1759, although one review[27] which appeared the following March is known to be his.

Samuel Johnson, also, may have been writing for the *Critical* much earlier than his biographers have thought. Late in 1758 Smollett writes to David Wilson, a printer, "I will take care of Mr. Johnson's papers and link them up in a very little time."[28] Noyes is puzzled by this statement and says, "According to Boswell's careful bibliography, Samuel Johnson was at this time writing nothing to which this statement could apply." It may be, however, that the "papers" which Smollett undertook to "link up" for Johnson were parts of a review. This is possible because, throughout the first thirty years of the *Critical,* extracts made up a large part of almost every long review, and these extracts were probably set up from the original copy, where possible, to save paying author's rates for straight copying.

In *The Battle of the Reviews* (1760), the two leaders of the *Critical* faction are "Sampson MacJackson" and "Sawney Mac-Smallhead." Smollett's biographers are agreed that the novelist is intended by "MacSmallhead," and it seems probable that "Sampson MacJackson" refers to the author of the *Dictionary.* Whether this is the intended reference, and, if so, whether the anonymous author of *The Battle* was well informed as to the identity of the editorial staff of the *Critical,* it now seems impossible to determine. The articles which have been ascribed to Johnson[29] do not appear until April, 1763, and the last quarter of 1764. In 1759 Smollett had enlisted the aid of Wilkes in returning Johnson's servant, who had run away and signed articles in the navy, and

---

[27] Of William Dunkin's *An Epistle to the Earl of Chesterfield,* in IX, 246–247.
[28] *Letters,* p. 52. The comment which follows is from p. 170.
[29] In W. P. Courtney and D. Nichol Smith, *A Bibliography of Samuel Johnson* (London, 1925), pp. 102–103.

the novelist writes to his future opponent on the *North Briton:* "I saw a very petulant card which he [Johnson] had sent to the Printer concerning an Article in the last *Review.*"[30]

The third of the most famous, besides Smollett, of the *Critical* contributors is David Hume, the historian. In April, 1759, a letter from Hume appears[31] as criticism of the second edition of Wilkie's *Epigoniad,* which had been roughly handled the year before. Boswell quotes Johnson in reference to reviews written by friends of the authors as follows.

He said the Critical reviewers on occasion of he and Goldsmith doing something together (i.e., publishing each a book at the same time, Mr. Johnson the *Idler*), let them know that they might review each other. Goldsmith was for accepting. He said "No. Set them at defiance."[32]

In view of this contribution by Hume, as well as the fact that other articles are known to have been written by friends of the authors reviewed, it is impossible to take seriously the *Critical's* assertion made in reply to Boswell's *Journal:* "We have never permitted friends to review each other's works."[33]

These men, with Robertson, Francklin, Mallett, Jones, John Campbell,[34] and James Ferguson,[35] comprise the majority of the

[30] *Letters,* p. 58.

[31] Hume may have written the review of Robertson's *History of Scotland,* which appears in VII (Feb., 1759), 89–103.

[32] *Journal of a Tour to the Hebrides with Samuel Johnson,* ed. Pottle and Bennet (New York, 1936), p. 239. The editors of the *Journal* consider this to refer to the first collected edition of the *Idler,* which was published in 1761. Iolo A. Williams, *Seven XVIIIth Century Bibliographies* (London, 1924), assigns no books to Goldsmith from December, 1759, to February, 1762.

[33] LX (Nov. 1785), 337.

[34] In November, 1762, Boswell wrote in his Journal (Cf. Malahide papers, p. 127) that Francklin and Campbell were writers on the *Critical.* This seems probable, inasmuch as the latter worked with Smollett on the *Modern Part of the Universal History* in 1760. No articles in the *Review* have been identified as his. Campbell may, however, be the person referred to in a letter from Hamilton quoted in the article on Smollett in Chamber's *General Biographical Dictionary:*

"Paunceford [in *Humphrey Clinker*] was a John C—l, who was fed by Smollett when he had not bread to eat, nor clothes to cover him. He was taken out to India [Campbell was sent to Georgia for writing a pamphlet on the West Indies and dedicating it to Lord Bute, Smollett's patron] as private secretary to a celebrated governor-general, and as essayist; and after two or three years absence returned with forty thousand pounds. From

writers who have been identified as *Critical* reviewers during our period. Even with our limited knowledge, we thus recognize contributors who are much more important than their rivals on the *Monthly*. Further, we may assume that Smollett was responsible for the presence of several of these men on the *Review* roster, that through his hands passed most of the material which they and others submitted to the journal during its first seven years. This would be reason enough for keeping alive the memory of a smaller man. But Smollett's *Critical* work has, until now, been almost completely submerged in the stream of his multifarious accomplishments. It should not be forgotten, however, that in addition to his worth as novelist, historian, party journalist, and minor poet, Smollett attained noteworthy stature as editor of the *Critical Review*.

India he sent several letters to Smollett, professing that he was coming over to lay his fortune at the feet of his benefactor. But on his arrival he treated Smollett, Hamilton, and others who had befriended him, with the most ungrateful contempt. . . . He died, in two or three years after, at his house near Hounslow, universally despised. At the request of Smollett, Mr. Hamilton employed him to write in the Critical Review, which, with Smollett's charity, was all his support previously to his departure for India."

[35] For Ferguson's connection with the *Review,* see the statement by the editors, XV (June, 1763), 409–421; and letters in XVI (Oct., 1764), 339–352.

APPENDIXES

Appendix A

In May, 1758, Smollett wrote for the *Critical*[1] the following review of *The Conduct of Admiral Knowles on the Late Expedition Set in a True Light,* London, 1758. It was this article which led to the novelist's imprisonment in the King's Bench in the following year.

If Vice Admiral K—s had recollected a certain unsavoury proverb, perhaps, he would have saved himself the trouble of stirring up the remembrance of a dirty expedition, which has stunk so abominably in the nostrils of the nation; he might likewise have been more cautious of disturbing the quiet in which has own character was suffered to rest. But some people are born for action, and would rather run the risque of hurting themselves, than allow their meddling talents to rust in idleness. It must be owned, however, for the honour of the gentleman whose work is under consideration, that though no man was ever involved in a greater number of scrapes and perplexities, yet he has always disengaged himself with a dexterity of address peculiar to himself. He has been compared to a cat, which, though thrown from the top of a house in twenty different attitudes, will always light on its feet; and to the arms of the Isle of Man, which are three legs conjoined in ham, inscribed *quocunque scieris stabo.* We have heard of a man who, without birth, interest, or fortune, has raised himself from the lowest paths of life to an eminent rank in the service; and if all his friends were put to the strappado, they could not define the quality or qualities to which he owed his elevation. Nay, it would be found upon enquiry, that he neither has, or ever had any friend at all; (for we make a wide distinction between a patron and a friend;) and yet for a series of years, he has been enabled to sacrifice the blood, the treasure, and the honour of his country, to his own ridiculous projects. Ask his character of those who know him, they will not scruple to say, he is an admiral without conduct, an engineer without knowledge, an officer without resolution, and a man without veracity. They will tell you he is an ignorant, assuming, officious, fribbling pretender; conceited as a peacock, obstinate as a mule, and mischievous as a monkey; that in every station of life he has played the tyrant with his inferiors, the incendiary among his equals, and commanded a sq—n occasionally for twenty years, without having even established his reputation in the article of personal courage. If the service can be thus influenced by caprice, admiral K—s needs not be surprised at his being laid aside after forty years constant and faithful service.

The design of this pamphlet is to vindicate himself from an implicated charge contained in the report of the board of inquiry, concerning the last expedition to the coast of France. It is there said, that the design of attack-

[1] V, 438–439.

ing Fort Fouras was laid aside upon the representation of vice-admiral Knowles, that the ship intended for that service was on ground at the distance of four or five miles from the shore. Mr. Knowles had, in our opinion, proved that this ship was actually on shore, as were also the bomb-ketches and the Coventry Frigate. It likewise plainly appears, that one of these bomb-ketches was actually conducted by the pilot Thierry; that the master of the Barfleur sounded the river *Charente* from bank to bank; and that the service was retarded but three hours by Thierry's being sent to chace in the Magnanime. He has given some reasons (tho' to us not satisfactory) for the fort being built on the shore without gunshot of the channel; he labours hard to prove that the Fort Fouras was inaccessible by sea, and, with respect to the report of captain Colby's offering to carry in the Princess Amelia, says, it is a mystery that may be unriddled by a monosyllable, that may be guessed at without explanation. But after all these demonstrations, we find that no person sounded nearer than three quarters of a mile of the fort; and whether the channel was not within that distance, is still a point far from being ascertained. In the name of heaven! why was all this space left untried? If the persons employed on this service were afraid of approaching nearer the fort in the day, they might have, with great safety, executed the design in the night. They might have foreseen their omission in this particular would leave the most material point undecided, and consequently subject them to doubts, suspicion, and censure. The most valuable part of this pamphlet is the affixed carte of the road of Basque, with the different soundings of the coast marked by figures.

Appendix B1

ATTACKS ON THE "CRITICAL," 1756–1771

An Abstract from the Monthly Critical Review. London, 1756.

Additional Articles. (See under Cleland, John)

The Adventures of an Author. 2 vols. London, 1767. (XXIII:216–217)[1]

"Amicus Amico," *pseud.* (See under The Critical Reviewers Criticised)

Anecdotes of Polite Literature. 4 vols. London, 1764. (XVII:434–442)

[Anstey, Christopher]. The Patriot, a Pindaric Address. 2d ed. London, 1768. (XXV:151)

An Appeal to the Public from the Malicious Misrepresentations of the Anonymous Fabricators of the Critical Review. London, 1770.

An Appendix to the Critical Review of March Last. London, 1758. (V: 78–79)

An Appendix to the Occasional Critic. (See under Shebbeare, John)

"The author of the Observer observed," *pseud.* (See under Huggins, William)

The Battle of the Reviews. London, 1760.

Bisset, Charles. Candid and Satisfactory Answers to the Several Suggestions of the Critical Reviewers on an Essay on the Medical Constitution of Great Britain. London, 1763.

Bowyer, William. A letter in *The Saint James Chronicle,* Oct. 8, 1767.

[Bridges, Thomas]. Homer Travestie. By Cotton Jr. London, 1762. (XIII: 519)

Browne, William. Appendix ad Opuscula. London, 1770. (XXI:74)

Canning, George. An Appeal to the Public from the Malicious Misrepresentations of the Critical Reviewers. London, 1767.

Caswall, Thomas. The Trifler; a Satire. London, 1766. (XXII:470–471)

Churchill, Charles. The Apology, addressed to the Critical Reviewers. London, 1761. (XI:409–411)

——. The Author. London, 1763.

——. The Candidate. London, 1764.

——. An Epistle to William Hogarth. London, 1763.

——. The Ghost. 2 vols. London, 1762–1763.

——. Gotham. 3 vols. London, 1764. (XVII:288–292)

[Cleland, John]. Additional Articles of an Etymological Vocabulary. London, 1769. (XXVIII:78)

The Coach Drivers; a Political Comic Opera. To which is Subjoined a Letter of Thanks to the Compilers of the Critical Review. London, 1766. (XXII:382)

---

[1] The numbers in parentheses refer to the volume and page number where comment on the item appears in the *Critical.*

Comber, Thomas. A Vindication of the Great Revolution in England. London, 1758. (V:236–239)

The Coteries Recommended; or the Pleasures of the Beau Monde Vindicated. By the Honourable Mr. Shandy. London, 1771. (XXXI:404)

"Cotton Jr.," *pseud*. (See under Bridges, Thomas)

"The Critical Review," in *Gentleman's Mag*. XXVI (March, 1756), 141–142. Quoted verbatim in *Scots Mag*. XVIII (1756), 156. (I:[287]–288)

The Critical Reviewers Criticised. I [no more published]. By Amicus Amico. London, 1761. (XII:318)

The Critical Reviewers Criticised and Lashed with Their Own Rods. By Amicus Amico. London, 1767.

"Crito," *pseud*. A letter in *Lloyd's Chronicle,* Sept. 10, 1764. (XVII:80)

"Curl, Edmund," *pseud*. (See under Smart, Christopher)

A Defence of Mr. Kenrick's Review of Dr. Johnson's Shakespeare. London, 1765. (XXI:79)

Dialogues of the Living. London, 1762. (XIII:519–520)

Extract of a Private Letter to a Critic. London, 1764. (XVII:320)

Fables for Grown Gentlemen. (See under Hall-Stevenson)

Farmer, Richard. The Learning of Shakespeare. 2d ed. London, 1767. (XXIV:400)

Foote, Samuel. The Lyar; a Comedy. London, 1764. (XVIII:120–124)

Fortescue, John. Dissertations, Essays, and Discourses. 2 vols. London, 1759. (VIII:137–143)

Freeman, George. Day; an Epistle to Dr. Churchill. London, 1762. (XIII: 362)

"From Edmund Curl . . ." (See under Smart, Christopher)

Goldsmith, Oliver. An Enquiry into the Present State of Polite Learning in Europe. London, 1761. (VII:369–372)

Grainger, James. A Letter to Tobias Smollett, M.D. Occasioned by his Criticism upon a Translation of Tibullus. London, 1759. (VII:141–158)

[Greene, Edward B.]. The Laureat; a Poem. London, 1765. (XIX:87–90)

[Hall-Stevenson, John]. Fables for Grown Gentlemen. London, 1770. (XIX:72–73)

[Hall-Stevenson, John]. A Nosegay and a Simile for the Reviewers; a Lyric Epistle. London, 1763.

"A Halter-Maker," *pseud*. (See under Reed, Joseph)

Henderson, Andrew. The Life of William the Conqueror. London, 1764. (XVIII:74)

[Hill, Richard]. Pietas Oxoniensis. 2d ed. London, 1768. (XXVI:318)

The History of the Sumatrans. (See under Shebbeare, John)

Homer Travestie. (See under Bridges, Thomas)

[Huggins, William]. A letter, signed "The author of the Observer observed," in *The General Evening Post,* June 15, 1756. (I:484)

Jones, Rowland. The Philosophy of Words. London, 1769. (XXVIII:77–78)

[Kenrick, William]. A Scrutiny; or, the Critics Criticised. London, 1759. (VII:88)

The Laureat. (See under Greene, Edward B.)

A Letter to the Author of the Critical Review. London, 1757.

A Letter to the Critical Review. London, 1760.

A Letter to the Critical Review. (See under N., M.)

[Lloyd, Evan]. The Powers of the Pen; a Poem. London, 1766. (XXI: 153–154)

Louisa; or, Virtue in Distress. London, 1760. (IX:318–319)

Mariott, Thomas. The Twentieth Epistle of Horace Modernized. London, 1759. (VIII:84–86)

"Mercurius Aspar," *pseud*. (See under Shaw, Cuthbert)

Miscellanies; the Lion, Cock, and Peacock; a Fable. London, 1767. (XXIV: 226)

A Mirror for Critics. By an Oxfordshire ploughman. London, 1762. (XIV: 319)

Mozeen, Thomas. Fables in Verse. 2 vols. London, 1765. (XX:171–176)

Murphy, Arthur. A Poetical Epistle to Samuel Johnson. London, 1760. (X: 319–320)

[N., M.] A Letter to the Critical Review. London, 1759. (VII:453–457)

Nihell, Elizabeth. An Answer to the Author of the Critical Review. London, 1760. (IX:412)

A Nosegay and a Simile for the Reviewers. (See under Hall-Stevenson, John)

Observations on the Account Given of the Catalogue of Royal and Noble Authors of England . . . in the Critical Review. London, 1759. (VII:179)

The Occasional Critic. (See under Shebbeare, John)

"An Oxfordshire ploughman," *pseud*. (See under A Mirror for Critics)

Parsons, James. A Letter in *The General Evening Post*, Sept. 15, 1756. (II: 188–192)

The Patriot. (See under Anstey, Christopher)

Patten, Thomas. St. Peter's Christian Apology. London, 1756. (II:144–155)

The Peregrinations of Jeremiah Grant. London, 1762. (XV:13–21)

Phillips, Thomas. A History of the Life of Reginald Poole. II. London, 1764. (XIX:17–27)

A Poem sacred to the Memory of William Beckford. London, 1770. (XXX: 74–75)

A Poetical Epistle to ———. (See under Woodhull, Michael)

The Powers of the Pen. (See under Lloyd, Evan)

The Public Advertiser, Jan. 14, 1771. [Unsigned letter]

The Race. (See under Shaw, Cuthbert)

[Reed, Joseph]. A Sop in the Pan for a Physical Critic: in a Letter to Dr. Sm[o]ll[et]t. By a Halter-Maker. London, 1759.

Remarks on Mr. Robert Dossie's Institutes of Experimental Chemistry. London, 1760. (IX:237–238)

"S.," *pseud.* (See under True Merit.)

The Saint James Chronicle, March 12, 1771. [Unsigned letter]. (XXXI: 315)

"Shandy," *pseud.* (See under The Coterie Recommended.)

[Shaw, Cuthbert]. The Race. By Mercurius Aspar. London, 1766. (XXI: 315)

[Shebbeare, John]. An Appendix to the Occasional Critic. London, 1759.

[Shebbeare, John]. The History of the Sumatrans. II. London, 1763. (XV: 209–210)

[Shebbeare, John]. The Occasional Critic, or the Decrees of the Scotch Tribunal Rejudged. London, 1757. (IV:332)

Sketches and Characters. (See under Thickness, Philip)

[Smart, Christopher]. "From Edmund Curl to the author of a thing called The Critical Review," in *The Universal Visiter and Monthly Memorialist,* I (March, 1756), 139–140. [See Appendix B2.]

Smart, Christopher. Poems. London, 1763.

Thicknesse, Philip. Observations on the Customs and Manners of the French Nation. London, 1766. (XXII:433–434)

[Thicknesse, Philip]. Sketches and Characters of the Most Eminent and Most Singular Persons Now Living. I. Bristol, 1770. (XXI:239–240)

[Thicknesse, Philip]. Useful Hints for Those Who Make the Tour of France. London, 1768. (XXV:277–284)

[Thompson, Edward]. Trinculo's Trip to the Jubilee. London, 1769. (XXVIII:378)

The Triumverate. By Veritas. London, 1761. (XII:318–319)

True Merit, True Happiness. Memoirs of Mr. S. 2 vols. London, 1756. (III: 467)

Two Letters to the Reviewers Occasioned by the Account of a Book Called Memoirs. London, 1760.

Tyburn to the Marine Society; a Poem. London, 1759. (VII:465)

Underwood, Thomas. A Word to the Wise; a Poetical Farce, most respectfully addressed to the Critical Reviewers. London, 1770. (XXIX:316)

"Veritas," *pseud.* (See under The Triumverate)

A Very Old Thing. London, 1768. (XXV:468)

Walpole, Horace. Anecdotes of Painting in England. 2d ed. 4 vols. London, 1767. (XXIV:56–58)

[Woodhull, Michael]. A Poetical Epistle to ——. London, 1761. (XII:236)

Appendix B2

The following letter, which may have been written by Christopher Smart, appeared in *The Universal Visiter and Monthly Memorialist* for March, 1756. I include it here because of its rarity; the only known copy of the magazine in this country is in the John Freeland Library, in New Orleans.

From Edmund Curl, *to the principal Author of a Thing,* called *the* Critical Review.
By favour of Mr. *Bencraft.*

Dear *JACKY,*[1]

For so I must style thee, though, to my extreme mortification, I had not even a personal knowledge of thee whilst I was bustling above stairs in the busy world. And here I cannot but marvel at the caprice of destiny, that a fellow, who spent so much of his life in and about Covent-Garden, should never find his way into Rose-street, where I constantly kept a pack of hungry creatures in pay, who would have been proud of his company and glad of his assistance. There were Mr. Joseph Gay, Mr. Thomas Pope, Mr. John Swift, and Mr. Richard Congreve, who would undoubtedly have deemed it an honour to have been acquainted with an hug-bug-rub-drug, pug-scrub, Axad. &c. Soc. The choice spirits, that have lately made their appearance in these parts, are full of your praises; and indeed, if what they say is true, you are justly the wonder of the world. A man who dresses like a gentleman, has the equipage of a gentleman, drinks and wenches like a gentleman, without any finances whatever, is certainly a greater object of admiration, than a man of real fortune that does all these things. In like manner, he who is a critic without taste, genius, judgement, learning, candour, or common sense, has doubtless infinitely more merit, than he who is possessed of these ingredients, and acts from the result of natural causes. Go on, great sir, and continue to deserve and receive the protection and encouragement of my worthy representatives yet on earth; and now and then, amidst your jollity, do not forget to fill a bumper to the glorious and immortal memory of

Your deceased admirer,

EDMUND CURL.[2]

---

[1] Probably "Jacky" refers to John Hill, who, although he evidently had nothing to do with the *Critical,* was thought by some of the opponents of the *Review* to be one of the editors.

[2] I, 139–140. This is in answer to the *Critical* article concerning the *Visiter* (I [Jan. and Feb., 1756], 85–88) which was decidedly unfavorable.

Appendix C

"THE UNFORTUNATE LOVERS"

The following story appeared for the first time in *The British Magazine* for May, 1760.[1] In the following month it was reprinted by *The Scots Magazine,* a monthly begun in 1739 and modeled on *The Gentleman's,* which also contains several other hitherto unnoticed items concerning Smollett. In its pages are reprinted *A North Briton Extraordinary,* which has been ascribed to Smollett;[2] at least three of his poems: "A new song,"[3] "Ode addressed to the late Gen. Wolfe,"[4] "Ode to Sleep;" several numbers of *The Briton;*[5] as well as extracts from his histories.[6]

In addition to these, there is a poem by "D. R———E" entitled "To Mr. T——S——, on his going abroad."[7] This may well have been written by Smollett's very good friend, Ritchie, when on April 3, 1740, the novelist was entered on H.M.S. *Chichester* for the Cartagena expedition. Another interesting contribution to the *Scots* during Smollett's lifetime is the series of eleven satires, printed during 1763 and 1764, as "By Dr. S."[8]

Twenty-seven years after its first appearance, Smollett's story was resurrected by the editor of *The New Novelists' Magazine, or Entertaining Library,*[9] who accredits it to Smollett, and gives the story a title.

Gentlemen;   Dorsetshire, April 28, 1760.

Give me leave, through the canal of your magazine, to communicate a story, which is not more romantic than true; and may serve as a lesson of prudence and morality to those parents, who think there is nothing but affluence necessary or essential to the happiness of their children.

---

[1] I, 121–125. It appears in the *Scots,* XXII, 303–305.

[2] See F. A. Pottle, "A North Briton Extraordinary," in *NQ,* CXVII (Oct. 11 and Dec. 6, 1924), 259 ff. The pamphlet is printed *in extenso* in the *Scots,* XXVII (1765), 134–138.

[3] XVII (1755), 446. See Howard Swazey Buck, *Smollett as a Poet* (New Haven and London, 1927), pp. 48–49. The song first appeared in *Roderick Random,* chap. 61.

[4] XXII (1760), 32. See Buck, *op. cit.,* pp. 63–68. The "Ode to Sleep" appears in XXII (1760), 315.

[5] All in XXIV (1762) as follows: No. 1, p. 286; No. 2, pp. 290–291, 394; No. 3, pp. 350–351; No. 4, p. 353.

[6] See XIX (1757), 662–663; XX (1758), 129–131, 225–238, 695–696.

[7] XI (1749), 164. Concerning Smollett's close friend, Ritchie, see *Letters,* pp. 5, 115.

[8] The verses appeared as follows: "To the memory of William Shenstone, Esq.," XXV (1763), 162; "Ode to Spring," *ibid.,* 346; "Satire" ("Yes, Zephalinda fair would wed ...") *ibid.,* 506; "The Monopolist," *ibid.,* 618; "Lauria," *ibid.,* 675–676; "Flavia and Lucia," XXVI (1764), 40; "To Miss J——y T——t——r," *ibid.;* "Epigram" ("How proud this rule adorns each shelf ..."), *ibid.;* "Stella," *ibid.,* 95–96; "Epitaphs on a miser," *ibid.,* 94; "The advantage of rhyming," *ibid.,* 151–154.

[9] I (1787), 24–27. Another story, with the same name, had appeared in *The Westminster Magazine,* IV (1776), 17–20.

Alcanor was the son of a London merchant, bred up to the business of his father, to which he succeeded in his early youth; and in little time distinguished himself, not only by his knowledge in trade, but also by his probity of heart, and generosity of sentiment. Nor was he deficient in personal accomplishments: his figure was remarkably agreeable; his address was engaging; and no pains had been spared in giving him the advantage of a genteel education.

He was in a fair way of acquiring a very large fortune, when he first beheld, at a public assembly, the elegant and amiable Eudosia, daughter of an eminent trader, to whom his circumstances were well known. He was deeply struck with her external appearance; and, having found means to insinuate himself into her acquaintance, discovered a thousand charms in her understanding and disposition, which at once completed the conquest of his heart. It was not long before he disclosed his passion to the dear object, and had the ravishing pleasure to find he had inspired her with very favourable sentiments of his character.

After some time spent in the endearing effusions of mutual love, he applied to the father, and made a formal demand of her in marriage. His proposal met with a very cordial reception; and Alcanor was admitted into the family on the footing of a future son-in-law. The day was already appointed for the marriage, after all the articles of interest had been settled to the satisfaction of both parties, when, by the sudden failure of foreign correspondence at the close of the last war, Alcanor was obliged to stop payment. He communicated his distress to Eudosia's father; and produced his books, by which it appeared that his effects were more than sufficient to discharge his debts; though they were so scattered, that he could not call them in time enough to support his credit. The merchant said he was sorry for his misfortune, but made no offer of assistance: on the contrary, he told him bluntly, that he could not expect he would bestow his daughter on a bankrupt, and forbad him the house. The reader may conceive what effect this treatment had upon an ingenious mind, indued with an extraordinary share of sensibility: he retired to his own house, his heart bursting with grief and indignation. The generous Eudosia, being apprised of what had passed between her father and her lover, seized the first opportunity of writing a letter to Alcanor, lamenting his misfortune in the most pathetic terms; assuring him of her inviolable attachment, and offering to give a convincing proof of her love by a clandestine marriage. He made due acknowledgements to his amiable mistress for this mark of her disinterested affection; but absolutely refused to comply with a proposal which might ruin her fortune, endanger her happiness, and subject him to the imputation of being sordid and selfish. He made haste to settle his accounts, and satisfy his creditors. Then he wrote a letter to Eudosia, releasing her from all engagements in his favour, and exhorting her to forget that ever any such person existed. Immediately after this address, he disappeared, and no person could tell in what manner: people, in general, supposed he had made away with himself in despair. Eudosia was overwhelmed with the most poignant sorrow, which entailed upon her a lingering distemper, that brought her to the brink of the grave. Though nature triumphed over the disease, it was not in the power of time to remove her grief, which settled into a fixed melancholy that clouded all her charms, and made a deep impression on her father's heart. Her only brother dying of a consumption, she became the sole heiress of a considerable fortune; and many advantageous matches were proposed without effect. At length, she plainly told her father, that he had once made her miserable, and it was not now in his power to make her happy; for she had made a solemn vow to heaven, that she would never join her fate to any other man but him on whom he had allowed her to bestow her affection. The merchant was thunderstruck at this declaration; he saw himself deprived, by his own cruel avarice, of that happiness which he had flattered himself with the hope of enjoying in a rising generation of his own posterity; he became pensive and sullen; lost his senses; and in a few months, expired.

Eudosia purchased a retired house in this neighbourhood, where she gave a full scope to her sorrow, while she lived the life of a saint, and spent the best part of her time, as well as fortune, in the exercise of charity and benevolence: witness the sighs that are still uttered by all that knew her, when her name is pronounced; witness the tears of the widow and the fatherless, that are daily shed upon her tomb.

Alcanor, desperate in his fortune and his love, took a passage in a Spanish ship for Cadiz, under the name of Benson; and as he understood the languages, as well as the management of accompts, he was admitted, as an inferior factor, on board of the Flota bound for South America. He settled at La Vera Cruz; and fortune so prospered his endeavours, that in a few years he was master of forty thousand pistoles. But neither prosperity nor the universal esteem he had acquired among the Spanish for his worth and integrity, could soothe the anguish of his heart, or efface the remembrance of Eudosia, whose charms still dwelt in his imagination. At length, impatient of living so long in ignorance of her situation, he remitted his effects to Europe, returned to Cadiz, and there, in a British bottom took shipping for England. At the Race of Portland the ship was attacked by a paultry French privateer, and Alcanor had the misfortune to receive a shot in his neck, which appeared very dangerous. After the privateer had sheered off, he desired that he might be put ashore at the nearest land, as there was no surgeon aboard, and the boat immediately conveyed him and part of his baggage into a creek, within half a mile of Eudosia's dwelling.

He was obliged to take up his lodging at a wretched public house, and dispatched an express to the next town for a surgeon; but before he arrived, the unfortunate Alcanor had lost his eyesight, in consequence of his wound, and his fever was considerably increased. The humane Eudosia, being made acquainted with the circumstances of his distress, without dreaming that it was her beloved Alcanor, desired a worthy old clergyman, who was rector of the parish, to take her chariot, and bring the wounded gentleman to her house, where he might be properly attended and accommodated. Thither he was carried accordingly, and there first visited by the surgeon, who, after having dressed the wound, declared he had no hopes for his recovery. He heard this sentence without emotion; and desired he might have an opportunity to thank the lady of the house for the charitable compassion she had manifested towards a stranger in distress.

The tender-hearted Eudosia, being informed of his request, immediately visited him in his apartment, accompanied by the clergyman, and a female relation who lived with her as her companion. Approaching his bedside, she condoled with him on his misfortune, begged he would think himself at home and command everything in her house as freely as if it were his own. He no sooner heard her voice than he started; and raising himself in his bed rolled his eyes around as if in quest of some favourite object. His ear was more faithful than his memory; he remembered and was affected by the strain, though he could not recollect the ideas to which it had been annexed: after some pause, he exclaimed, "Excellent lady! I could wish to live, in order to express my gratitude: but it will not be—you have given shelter to a poor wearied pilgrim; and your charity must be still farther extended in seeing his body committed to the dust. I have, moreover, another favour to ask, namely, that you and this good clergyman will attest my last will, which is locked in a paper case deposited in my portmanteau." So saying, he delivered the key to the doctor, who opened the trunk, found the paper, and was desired to recite it aloud in the hearing of all present. The will was written by the hand of Alcanor himself, who, in consideration of his tender affection for the incomparable Eudosia, which nothing but death could eraze from his heart, had bequeathed to her all his worldly substance, exclusive of some charitable legacies. When the name of Alcanor was pronounced, Eudosia started, grew pale, and trembled with strong emotion: yet she considered his situation, and restrained her transports, while her eyes poured forth a torrent of tears, and the chair shook under her with the violence of her agony. The humane clergyman was not unmoved at this scene. He had often heard the story of her unfortunate love, and by his sensible consolations enabled her to bear her affliction with temper and resignation. He no sooner perceived the names of Alcanor and Eudosia in the will, than he was seazed with extreme wonder, and sympathetic sorrow. His voice faltered; the tears ran down his cheeks—and it was with the utmost difficulty that he read the paper to an end. Then observing the agitation of Eudosia, he conducted her into another room, where, her grief and surprize becoming too strong for her constitution, she fainted away in the arms of her companion. When she recovered from the swoon, she gave vent to her sorrow in a loud passion of tears and exclamation: after which she became more calm, and begged the doctor would endeavour to prepare Alcanor for an interview with his long-lost Eudosia. He forthwith returned to the merchant; but was in too much confusion to communicate the discovery with discretion and composure.

Alcanor, though blind, had perceived the lady's agitation, as well as the clergyman's disorder, and was not a little surprised at their abrupt departure. His mind had already formed an assemblage of the most interesting ideas before the doctor returned; and when he began to expatiate the mysterious way of Providence, he was interrupted by the stranger, who, raising his head, and clasping his hands, exclaimed aloud, "O bountiful Heaven! it must—it must be the incomparable Eudosia!" At that instant she entered the apartment, kneeled by the bedside, and taking him by the hand, "It is (cried she) the unfortunate Eudosia—O my Alcanor! Is it thus we meet?" A long silence ensued, during which he bathed her hand with his tears,—At length he spoke to this effect: "These are not the tears of sorrow but of joy—Eudosia then lives! she remembers—she retains her regard for the hapless Alcanor?—it was indeed the kind hand of Providence that threw me on this hospitable shore—could I once more behold those dear features which I have so often contemplated with admiration and delight—but, I am satisfied."—The sequel of this affecting scene I cannot pretend to describe—Alcanor's wound at the next dressing had the appearance of a beginning gangrene; nevertheless, the ball which had been lodged among the nerves and sinews of the neck, was now with ease extracted, and his eyesight was immediately restored. Having settled his temporal affairs, and made his peace with heaven, he on the fourth day expired in the arms of Eudosia, who was the sole and last object on which his eyes were strained. She did not long survive her unfortunate lover.— Her grief at length exhausted her constitution, and brought her to the grave, after she had endowed alms-houses for the maintenance of twenty poor cripples, bequeathed a handsome fortune on her kinswoman: a considerable present to the clergyman, and a large sum to the poor of the parish. At her own desires she was buried in the same grave with her lover, and over them is raised a plain unembellished tomb of black marble, with this modest inscription: "Dedicated to the memory of ALCANOR and EUDOSIA."

I am, &c.

Appendix D

Appendix D

The following poem may have been inspired by Gray's "Ode on the Death of a Favourite Cat," which appeared in print for the first time in Dodsley's *Collection* in 1748. It is ascribed to Smollett by the Huntington Library cataloguers, and by Quaritch.[1] The exact reason for this ascription does not appear, however, but I reprint it here because, first, of its possible Smollett association; and, second, of its comments on Fielding, Lyttleton, and Young. The full title is as follows:

> A / Sorrowful DITTY; / or, the LADY's / LAMENTATION / For the DEATH / OF HER / FAVOURITE CAT. / A PARODY. / — / *Sequitur non passibus æquis*. VIRG. / — / LONDON: / Printed for J. Tomlinson, near St. *Paul's*. 1748.

The Huntington Library copy, from which the text here is taken, is in 4to, with the following pagination: [1–2; blank t.p. verso] 3–12.

I

Well! Thanks to my Stars! I'm at last all alone;
My Business and troublesom Visits are done:
Embower'd in this Closet, secure from Surprize,
Just Sorrow indulging, I'll cry out my Eyes:
This is the chief,
Sole Relief,
To my Grief;
Not caus'd by meer Trifles, inelegant, gross,
But Oh! my poor Puss! thy deplorable Loss.

II

Ye tufted Settees, and thou soft Elbow-Chair,
How oft on your Lapps has she purr'd away Care?
Ye Carpets gay smiling with yellow and red,
How oft has she press'd you with delicate Tread?
But again,
Can't be seen,
What has been;
For Night's sable Mantle around her is put,
And those beauteous Peepers for ever are shut.

---

[1] See Catalogue 546 (1938), item 605.

III

Both Wood-Lark and Linnets I cherish at home,
Sweet *Philomel* also hangs up in my Room;
Yet She, when for conjugal Mysteries ripe,
Could Silence 'em all with her Clearness of Pipe:
So acute,
Ev'ry Flute,
Was struck mute;
Which now may play on, and Those sing if they please,
Since Death has thought proper her Musick should cease.

IV

I take out my Glass, and with Diligence look,
Explore ev'ry Corner, and search ev'ry Nook:
Unwearied, from rising to setting of Sun,
In Quest of my dearest *Grimalkin* I run:
Still my Eye,
Can espy
Nothing nigh,
Save only the different Parts of the House,
Where dosing she watch'd the too credulous Mouse.

V

Meer Solitude now! Oh! for ever bemoan,
Ye desolate Walls, your Inhabitants flown!
Remember how modest her Charms! in her Breast
How Passion subsided, and all was at Rest!
Gaudy Courts,
Gay Resorts,
Pleasing Sports,
She view'd with Contempt; choosing here to retire,
And suckle her innocent Young by the Fire.

VI

Sweet Kittens! abandon'd, who sprawl on the Ground,
Where now shall Assistance to rear you be found?
What Mother so fond in her Bosom shall warm?
What Tongue new-creating shall lick into Form?
Alas none!
Sure as Gun,
You're undone;
And I wretch, I only am left to bewail
This double misfortune, and tell the dull Tale!

VII

How could you be gossiping then, Sisters nine,
When, gasping, her Life she was forc'd to resign?
Your Pray'rs might have mov'd the compassionate Gods,
And kept Her as yet from th' *Elysian* Abodes:
In my Mind,
'Twas unkind;
And you'll find,
Upon your Annals will ever remain,
This fatal Neglect, an indelible Stain.

VIII

But if coining Names for *Pelagius's* Work,
Or spinning an Ode from bright $J--n--gs^2$ to $Y--k;^3$
If teaching lank $L--tt-lt--n^4$ graceful to weep,
Or rocking poor supperless $F--ld--ng^5$ to sleep;
These I own,
Might atone,
For what's done:
Nor could less essential Reasons excuse
This shameful Desertion of every Muse.

IX

What tho' from the choicest of *Italy's* Throats,
My Concerts resound with melodious Notes;
What tho' the Politeness of Favourite *France*
Appears at each Ball, and enlivens the Dance;
Pleasure there,
Can I share?
No, my Fair,
Since Destiny thus thro' their Faults could prevail,
These many Advantages nothing avail.

---

[2] Soame Jenyns.
[3] Charles Yorke.
[4] George, first Baron Lyttleton, who when his wife died wrote a *Monody* which was ridiculed by Smollett in a burlesque ode in *Peregrine Pickle,* chap. 102.
[5] Henry Fielding.

X

To make Her some Recompense, Virgins, Oh! save
Her sweet smelling Name from Oblivion's dark Grave!
In pious regard to her Memory, come,
And with your good Companies honour her Tomb:
On the Wing,
Come and bring,
Flow'rs of Spring;
With these wreath'd in Garlands bedizen her Herse,
And sing her Parfections in durable Verse.

XI

The Catalogue follows—*Imprimis,* A Face
With Whiskers adorn'd, and peculiar Grace—
Two Eyes of exceeding fine Lustre—A Skin
Superbly enamel'd with Spots—Then within
Charms immense!
Such Pretence,
To good Sense!
So tender in Nature, no Victim could bleed,
Tho' doomed for her Prey, but she wept at the Deed!

XII

Did Fortune attack Her with Frowns or a Smile?
Ambition or Int'rest attempt to beguile?
In vain: To be moderate, prudent and wise,
Was her's, and the Follies of Life to despise.
Such she was,
When alas!
Dire Disgrace!
With foaming Rapidity boisterous Death,
Came on like a Torrent, and stopt her sweet Breath.

XIII

Pursuing his wanton Amusement, the Boy
Thus forms by Inflation a watery Toy;
Around the thin Convex, as skilful He plays,
A thousand bright Colours *Sol* paints with his Rays;
But at last,
Comes a Blast,
Blown too fast;
Nor ceases (ah, cruel!) its Bowels to tear,
'Till bursts the fine Bubble, and mounts into Air.

XIV

Haste hither, funereal *Y—n—g*,[6] from thy Seat,[7]
Where Tan Pits so fragrant invite a Retreat:
Bring with Thee, propitious, that leaden-ton'd Lyre,
Whose Strings, rightly tun'd, gloomy Horror inspire:
If I Play,
The sad Lay,
Will convey,
Sounds dismal enough to shock every Ear
And render inanimate all that shall hear.

XV

For sure the World's Sorrow, and Man's fickle State,
Are Nothings compar'd to my *Tabb's* wretched Fate
Tho' well you lament 'em, in what could They please,
Who never protected from Nibblers your Cheese?
Then with Head-
Ach in Bed,
Almost dead,
Who never whole Nights on your Pillow have lain,
Assuaging the Torment, and easing the Pain?

XVI

That Amorous Youth who enjoy'd his Belov'd
By *Venus* transform'd to a Virgin, yet prov'd
Less Transports than I of her Friendship possest,
The dearest Companion, of Creatures the best.
Her I mourn,
From me torn,
All Forlorn;
And tho' told I've Beauty, Wit, twenty fine Things,
Howe'er just the Praise is, no Comfort it brings.

XVII

Depriv'd of her Presence, nor Books, ancient Friends,
Nor former Amusements can make me amends.
So deep throbs the Wound in my dolorous Heart,
All Balsams are vain, ineffectual Art
Ev'ry Hour,
Shows the Power,
She'd o'er
My Senses; for all that I see, feel, or hear,
Reminds me of Tabby, and calls forth a Tear.

---

[6] Edward Young.   [7] At *Wellwyn,* next Door to a Tanner's Yard. [Author]

XVIII

Years rolling and smiling like Wave after Wave,
Still follow'd each other, and Happiness gave.
The Chain of harmonious Concord fast bound us,
Felicity skipt, and Joy danc'd all around us;
Was then not,
Hard my Lot,
That this Blot
Should come and deface so fair written a Leaf?
—Yet soft—too abundant perhaps flows my Grief.

XIX

She's blest, pleasing Thought! So contented am I:
But Oh! let her meet me when call'd to the Sky!
We'll then mount together, and close by the *Bear,*
In one Constellation each twinkle a Star:
As we blaze,
In amaze,
Men shall gaze;
And ever be pointing, "There shine from above,
"True Mirrours of Constancy, Patterns of Love."

FINIS

Appendix E

APPENDIX E

The two letters which follow were written to Smollett by a fellow Scot, Dr. John Gray, who became one of the novelist's close friends. He was author of *A History of the World* in 12 volumes (1767) and translator of Horace (1778). Lewis Benjamin reprints two of Gray's letters to Smollett,[1] but apparently he did not know of the ones here presented, which are in the collections of the Library Company of Philadelphia, to which I am indebted for permission to reproduce the texts.

i

Sir

The great & usefull work you have so successfully carry'd on to the present time has certainly familiariz'd you to a correspondence with Strangers. Yet perhaps I am not altogether a Stranger to You. I have heard you are one of that Society of Gentlemen who compose the Critical Review, and a Book which I published lately upon Landmeasuring, was favoured with the approbation of that & the Monthly Review. That noble Candour & impartiality which distinguish all Your Observations, particularly in the latter part of your History imbolden me to write to you. I have had another Publication ready these 18 months, of far greater consequence, and which, when order'd by the Commissioners appointed by Parliament for that purpose, will make a figure, I hope, in Your History. You are, no doubt, acquainted with several good Mathematicians & skillfull Navigators; be pleased then, Sir, to communicate to them the following short abstract of my Theory.

Let exact Tables be made of the Moon's Declination for 20 years, & also of it's Variation Daily Difference, for every Decad of Longitude: lett also an exact Table be made of the Declinations of about 40 fixed stars the difference of whose Right Ascensions does not exceed one hour: and let all the Declinations be found in Degrees, Minutes & Seconds of the First Meridian. The Declinations of the fixed Stars will be the same, any Night, upon any Meridian; and their Mer: Altitudes, in any Latitude, will always differ by their Declinations only. But the Mer. Altitudes of the Moon, in every Second of Latitude, on the first Meridian, any Night, will differ from those of the next Night, in the same places, by the whole daily Difference of the Declination; and on any other Meridian in the same Latitude, by a part of the Daily Difference proportional to the Equatorial Distance of That from the First Meridian. This Proportional Part may be found thus: Observe the Meridian Altitude of the Moon & and of your fixed Stars that culminates soon after (or before) any place; if their difference be exactly that of the Declinations, the place is under the First Meridian; but if it be more, or less, the excess, or deficiency is the Proportional Part

---

[1] *The Life and Letters of Tobias Smollett* (London [1926]), pp. 243–257.

required. The following Proportion therefore will hold. As the whole Daily Difference of Declination to 360°. So is the Proportional Part to the Longitude. And consequently the Variation of Declination for any Decad of Longitude To the Degrees in that Decad, so is the proportional Part to the Longitude. As I have [catchwords at end of page] As I have been a Teacher of Practical Mathematics for 20 Years, it may be supposed that I know Refractions, Parallaxes, Precession &c. To reduce the above Theory to Practice I have contrivd a new construction of a Quadrant, which, with a Radius of 16 Inches, distinguishes every Second by 1/28 of an Inch; & by which a Meridian Altitude may be taken, either by Land or Sea, more easily & surely than by any other Quadrant yet contrived. Any Objections that may be made against it must fall much heavier upon the Observations for the Altitude at Sea; to which notwithstanding, all our Navigators trust: consequently there is little or nothing in them. Notwithstanding the Moon's irregularities (another seeming objection) our best Geographies declare that an Eclipse of the Moon is an excellent Method to determine the Longitude at Land: but my method must be far more exact. Her Place can certainly be found to 6 Minutes, otherwise the Longitude at Land could not be found, by an Eclipse, to any exactness: but these 6 Min: will not make an Error of 2 Minutes in her Declination, and 1/36 of these 2 Min: is all that can affect my Method: & after trying, in vain, what could be done in this country to bring my Discovery to a fair hearing, at London, I sent, last month, a Copy of the Theory, suitably introduced, and more fully express'd, with the practical Rules deducible from it subjoin'd, to the following Gentlemen, who are appointed by Law Commissioners for the Discovery of the Longitude, viz To the First Commissioners of the Admiralty, Navy & Trade, Master of the Trinity House, President of the Royal Society, Royal Astronomer, Savilian, Lucasian & Plumian Professors of the Mathematics, & to Admiral Hawke, desiring to be called before them: I sent also One to the Rt. Honble. Jas Stuart Mackenzie; but have yet received no Answer from any of them. Very probably You, Sir, and your Mathematical Friends are acquainted with all or most of these Gentlemen; and I hope your Public Spirit will interest You in the cause of a Stranger Perhaps, by your means, They may be prevail'd on to consider the thing & send for me. Without a moral certainty of having justice done me, I cannot leave my business to come up: for if I leave my business, I lose my bread. The Gentlemen will probably shew you the Letters I wrote to them, and You may shew them this. Be pleased to direct to me Teacher of Mathematics in Cupar of Fife and give me leave to expect Your Answer with your first conveniency. I am very respectfully Sir

Your most humble Servant

Cupar 20th Octr. 1761.   JOHN GRAY

Dear Sir   Florence Novr. 18th 1770.

As I mentioned to you that I had attempted the translation & imitation of a french petite piece, I now trouble you with five or six of the songs, to have ye beneft of your criticisms & corrections. The piece pleased me very much in ye representation, which made me wish to see it, or something like it on our stage, never dreaming at that time that I should employ my time about it myself. But having little to do at Bordeaux & Marseilles, I attempted one or two songs, & one or two more at sea & at Naples till my eagerness after ye fine arts antient & modern at Rome, put a stop to all & I don't know when I shall resume ye subject. The songs are not in ye order of ye piece; but I have numbred them as they fall in; & as we have yearly so many imperfect sonnets that pass off, on account of ye music I would hope that ye same mantle might cloak ye imperfections of mine. Not but that I could wish to have them as perfect to ye public ear & eye as possible: I have here copied ye french that you may compare ye two & together . . . [I omit Gray's long transcription from the French; evidently his translations were written on a separate sheet, which has been lost.]

I have no idea whether it be good or bad. I do not know whether ye measure I have chosen will pass in English; But what would not be allowed in a long poem might be permitted in two stanzas. The french of ye last song here, which ought to precede what is called the third, and the *Duo,* is. Tout ce qui peut toucher une Ame,—Se reunit pour me charmer—Hereurs femme—Tout respire ici pout m'aimer. De sa l'Amour couronne Ma tendresse et mes desirs, et la chaine quil me donne—Est l'ouvrage de plaisirs. I thought ye idea of the four last lines would make but a bad figure in English and substituted something else for it.

(Secreto.) One of my friends & correspondents before I entered Italy begged of me when at Leghorn to enquire privately into ye character, I mean into ye credit and mercantile reputation of Fred. Honore Bert, or Berte, merchant or merchants in that City, I entirely forgot the Commission when at Leghorn; but should be much obliged to you if you could procure me some about the said Berte, that in some degree satisfy my Correspondent. You might perhaps in conversation with Mr. Renner, learn as if by accident all that is required.

I despaired of executing Mrs Smolletts Commission, for there was no ultramarine to be found in the shops but I at length procured a little from Mr. Patch, which I have sent along with the Patterns in Mrs Vanim's letter, hoping that the word *mostri* on the back of the letter, will serve for a passport to all. The Ultramarine costs nothing; therefore if it arrives safe the Commission is finished.

By ye dilatoriness of my tipling companion we were benighted before we reach'd Pisa; & at about half a mile from the city, we were overtaken by a terrible storm of thunder lightening & rain, when ye darkness was so great, that we were obliged to stop for half an hour, till we could get a bit of torch from a neighbouring hut, being obliged to quit the chaise in the heavy rain, for fear ye restless mules should push us into ditches on one side or into the Arno on the other; from which adventure I have had a kind of Rhumatic cold for these eight days past, which begins to now abate. The morning after my arrival at Pisa I employ'd three or four hours in viewing the Place, and as the situation seemed to me to point out a most easy & natural method for preventing the inundations of the Arno, I have since my return hither written a few pages on that subject, upon which I am told several engineers in Italy have been consulted. Experience & execution are ye only things that can justify plans of that kind; but from ye manner of proceeding of the present directors in regard to the river, it is evident enough that they are groping very sadly.—We have no fresh English news here, but what you have pre[sent (tear in MS)]ly at Leghorn; namely that ye Marquis of Granby is dead & that Admiral Knowles is entered into Russian service. The Marquis is said died of an Apoplexy at Scarborough from venturing into the sea, when somewhat overcharged with liquor. Knowles according to reports here is to have 2000 £ a year during actual service, & 1000 £ a year for life. The Czarina has sent great presents to ye Commanders of her fleet in ye Archipelago. 25,000 Robles and an order of knighthood to Admiral Greg; but nothing to Admiral Elphinston.

I beg to present my respects to Mrs. Smollett, and Mr. & Mrs. Renner, & to Miss Fanny, & am with the sincerest esteem

Dear Sir
Your most obedient and
most humble servant
J. GRAY

BIBLIOGRAPHY

BIBLIOGRAPHY

ANDERSON, J. P. A Smollett bibliography in David Hannay, *The Life of Tobias George Smollett*. London, 1887. Pp. i–x in back.

ANDERSON, ROBERT. A life of Smollett prefixed to *The Miscellaneous Works of Tobias Smollett*, I (Edinburgh, 1820), pp. 1–203.

Annual Register, The. I–XXVII (1759–1785).

[Anonymous.] "An account of the American troops at Carthagena," in *Proceedings of the Mass. Hist. Soc.*, XVIII (1881), 364–378. *An Account of the Expedition to Carthagena.* Edinburgh, 1743. *Ballads to Admiral Vernon.* London, 1741. *A Compleat History of the Present War with Spain.* London, 1742. *Considerations on the Bill for the Better Government of the Navy.* By a Sea-Officer. London, 1749. "Dr. Oliver Goldsmith," in *N. Y. Med. Journal*, CXII (Nov., 1920), 727–728. "Doctors in British fiction," in *British Med. Journal*, I (Jan. 3, 1903), 40–41. *Farces and Entertainments.* Edinburgh, 1793. *Hints for the more Efficiently Regulating . . . His Majesty's Navy.* By a Sea-Officer. London, 1758. "A journal of the expedition to Carthagena," in *Gent. Mag.*, XIV (April, 1744), 29–41, 207–211. "Letters from Jamaica dated March 14 [1742]," in *Gent. Mag.*, XII (June, 1742), 330. *The Naval History of Great Britain, with the Lives of the Most Illustrious Admirals and Commanders.* 4 vols. London, 1758. *Original Letters to an Honest Sailor* [i.e., Admiral Vernon]. London, 1746. "Our man-o'-war's men," in *Dublin Univ. Mag.*, XLVI (Dec., 1855), 649–663. *Reflections on Navall Discipline.* [*Ca.* 1690.] MS in New York Public Library. "Smollett in the South," in *All the Year Round*: reprinted in *Littell's Living Age*, CXCII (Feb. 20, 1892), 507–510. "Some medical worthies of Bath II," in *The Practitioner*, XXIII (Jan., 1906), 109–115. "Tobias Smollett," in *The Medical Journal and Record*, CXXIV (July 7, 1926), 42–43. "Tobias Smollett," in *Quarterly Rev.*, CIII (Jan., 1858), 66–108.

AYLWARD, W. J. "The old man-of-war's man," in *Scribner's*, XL (Jan., 1914), 30–45.

BALDERSTON, KATHERINE CANBY. *A Census of the Manuscripts of Oliver Goldsmith.* New York, 1926. *The History and Sources of Percy's Memoir of Goldsmith.* Cambridge [Eng.], 1926.

BARROW, JOHN. *The Life of George Lord Anson.* London, 1839.

BELJAME, ALEXANDRE. *Le Public et les hommes de lettres en Angleterre au dixhuitième siècle.* Paris, 1881.

Bell's British Theatre. London, 1780.

[BENJAMIN, LEWIS.] *The Life and Letters of Tobias Smollett (1721–1771).* By Lewis Melville [pseud.]. London, 1926.

Biographia Navalis. 4 vols. London, 1796.

BOSWELL, JAMES. *Journal of a Tour to the Hebrides with Samuel Johnson.* Ed. F. A. Pottle and C. H. Bennet. New York, 1936. *The Life of Samuel Johnson.* Ed. G. Berbeck Hill. 6 vols. London, 1887. *Private Papers of James Boswell from Malahide Castle.* 12 vols. Mt. Vernon, New York, 1928–1935.

BRIDGE, CYPRIAN. "Did Elizabeth starve her seamen?" in *Nineteenth Century*, L (Nov., 1901), 774–789.

British Magazine, The. I–XIII (1760–1767). All published.

Briton, The. I–II (1762–1763). All published.

BUCK, HOWARD S. "A Roderick Random play—1748," in *MLN*, XLIII (Feb., 1928), 111–112. "Smollett and Dr. Akenside," in *JEGPh*, XXI (Jan., 1932), 10–26. *Smollett as a Poet.* New Haven and London, 1927. *A Study in Tobias Smollett.* New Haven, 1925.

BULKELEY, JOHN, and CUMMINS, THOMAS. *A Voyage to the South Seas.* London, 1743.

BURROWS, MONTAGU. *The Life of Edward Lord Hawke.* London, 1883.

CALLENDER, G. A. R. *Sea Kings of Britain—Albermarle to Hawke.* London, 1909.

[CAMPBELL, ARCHIBALD.] *The Sale of Authors, a Dialogue*. London, 1767.

CANNING, GEORGE. *An Appeal to the Publick, from the Malicious Misrepresentations of the Critical Review*. London, 1767.

CHANCELLOR, E. B. "Smollett as traveller," in *Fortnightly Rev., N.S.*, CXV (March 1, 1921), 478–488.

CHARRIÈRE, JOSEPH DE LA. *A Treatise on the Operation of Surgery*. London, 1712.

CHILD, HAROLD. "Smollett," in *CHEL*, XIV, pp. 22–50.

CHURCHILL, CHARLES. *Poems*. 2 vols. London, 1765.

CLARKE, EARNEST. "The medical education and qualifications of Oliver Goldsmith," in *Proceedings of the Royal Society of Medicine*, VII (Jan. 28, 1914), 88–89. "Oliver Goldsmith as a medical man," in *Nineteenth Century*, LXXV (April, 1914), 821–831.

CLOWES, WILLIAM [and others]. *The Royal Navy*. 7 vols. Boston, 1897–1903.

COURTNEY, W. P., and SMITH, D. NICHOL. *A Bibliography of Samuel Johnson*. London, 1925.

CRANE, RONALD S., and KAYE, F. B. *A Census of British Newspapers and Periodicals 1620–1800*. Chapel Hill, 1927.

CRAWFORD, RAYMOND. "Oliver Goldsmith and medicine," in *Proc. Royal Soc. Med.*, VI (Dec., 1913), 233–237.

CREIGHTON, CHARLES. *A History of Epidemics in Britain*. 2 vols. Cambridge [Eng.], 1894.

Critical Review, The. I–LX (1756–1785).

CUMBERLAND, RICHARD. *The Brothers;* in Mrs. Inchbald, *The British Theatre*, Vol. XVIII. London, 1808.

DAVIS, JOHN. *The Post-Captain, or the Wooden Walls well manned*. London, 1928.

DIBDIN, THOMAS. *The Naval Pillar*. Dublin, 1800.

DOUGHTY, KATHARINE P. "The attack on Carthagena," in *United Service Mag.*, LVIII (Oct., 1918), 40–52.

DRINKER, CECIL K. "Doctor Smollett," in *Annals of the History of Medicine*, VII (March, 1925), 31–47.

ELLISON, L. M. "Elizabethan drama and the works of Smollett," in *PMLA*, XLIV (1929), 842–862.

ELOESSER, L. "Pirate and buccaneer doctors," in *Annals of Medical History*, VIII (March, 1926), 31–60.

ENTICK, JOHN. *A New Naval History: or Compleat View of the British Marine*. London, 1757.

FIELD, CYRIL. *Britain's Sea-Soldiers*. 2 vols. Liverpool, 1924.

FLETCHER, W. J. "The press gang," in *Nineteenth Century*, L (Nov., 1901), 761–773. "The traditional British sailor," in *Nineteenth Century*, XLVIII (Sept., 1900), 423–435.

FORD, DOUGLAS. *Admiral Vernon and the Navy*. London, 1907.

FORSTER, JOHN. *The Life and Times of Oliver Goldsmith*. 5th ed. London, 1871.

FORTESCUE, J. W. *A History of the British Army*. 2 vols. London, 1899.

FREEMANTLE, EDMUND. "Hawke," in *Sea Kings of Britain from Howard to Nelson*. Ed. John Laughton. London, 1899.

GARRISON, FIELDING H. *An Introduction to the History of Medicine*. New York, 1926.

Gentleman's Magazine, The. I–LXX (1731–1800).

GOLDSMITH, OLIVER. *The Collected Letters*. Ed. Katharine Balderston. Cambridge [Eng.], 1928. *New Essays*. Ed. R. S. Crane. Chicago, 1927. *The Works*. Ed. J. W. M. Gibbs. 5 vols. London, 1884–1886. *The History of England*. 4 vols. London, 1809.

GOSSE, PHILIP. *The Pirates' Who's Who*. Boston, 1924.

GRAHAM, R. B. CUNNINGHAME. *Doughty Deeds*. London, 1925.

GRAHAM, WALTER. *English Literary Periodicals*. New York, 1930.

GRAY, JOHN. Two letters to Tobias Smollett. MSS in Library Company of Philadelphia. (See Appendix E *supra*.)

Gray's Inn Journal, The. I–II (1753–1754). All published.

GREEN, ROBERT. "Tobias Smollett physician and novelist," in *Boston Med. and Surgical Journal*, CLXXI (Oct. 22, 1914), 635–638.

HALIFAX, GEORGE, MARQUIS OF. *A Rough Draft of a New Model at Sea;* reprinted in *Political Pamphlets*. Ed. A. F. Pollard. London, 1897, pp. 37–57.

HALL, CHARLES. *Cartagena, or the Lost Brigade*. Boston, 1898.

HANNAY, DAVID. *The Life of Frederick Marryatt*. London, 1889. *The Life of Tobias George Smollett*. London, 1887. "Navy and navies," in *Ency. Brit.*, 11th ed. "Smollett and the old sea dogs," in *Blackwood's Mag.*, CLXIV (Aug., 1898), 231–243.

HANNAY, JAMES. "Sea novels—Captain Marryatt," in *Cornhill*, XXVII (Feb., 1873), 170–190.

HASKELL, GLEN. "Picaresque Elements in Smollett's Novels." Unpub. dissertation. Syracuse [N.Y.] University, 1929.

HEAD, RICHARD, and KIRKMAN, FRANCIS. *The English Rogue*. London, 1928.

HERVEY, JOHN. *Memoirs of the Reign of George the Second*. 3 vols. London, 1884.

HUNTER, A. C. "Les livres de Smollett détenus par la douane à Boulogne en 1763," in *Rev. Litt. Comp.*, XI (Oct., 1931), 736–737.

INCHBALD, MRS., ed. *The British Theatre*. 25 vols. London, 1808. *A Collection of Farces and Afterpieces*. 7 vols. London, 1815.

JAMES, WILLIAM. *The Naval History of Great Britain, 1793–1820*. 5 vols. London, 1822.

JOLIAT, EUGÈNE. "Smollett, editor of Voltaire," in *MLN*, LIV (1939), 429–436.

JONES, CLAUDE E. "Christopher Smart, Richard Rolt and the *Universal Visiter*," in *Library*, XVIII (Sept., 1937), 212–214. "A Smollett Letter," in *MLN*, L (1935), 242–243. "A Smollett letter and a poem," in *NQ*, CLXXIV (Feb. 26, 1938), 152. "Tobias Smollett on the 'Separation of the pubic joint in pregnancy,'" in *Medical Life*, XLI (June, 1934), 302–305.

KAHRL, GEORGE M. "The influence of Shakespeare on Smollett," *Essays in Dramatic Literature* (ed. Hardin Craig). Princeton, 1935.

KNAPP, LEWIS M. "More Smollett letters," in *MLN*, XLVIII (1933), 246–249. "Naval scenes in 'Roderick Random,'" in *PMLA*, XLIX (1934), 593–597. "The publication of Smollett's *Complete History and Continuation*," in *Library*, XVI (Dec., 1935), 295–301. "Ralph Griffiths, author and publisher," in *Library*, XX (Sept., 1939), 197–213. "Smollett's early years in London," in *JEGPh*, XXXI (April, 1932), 220–227. "Smollett's works as printed by William Strahan, with an unpublished letter of Smollett," in *Library*, XIII (Dec., 1932), 282–291.

[KNOWLES, CHARLES.] *The Conduct of Admiral Knowles in the Late Expedition Set in a True Light*. London, 1758.

LEADAM, I. S. *The History of England . . . 1702–1760*. London, 1909.

LECKY, WILLIAM. *A History of England in the Eighteenth Century*. 7 vols. New York, 1878.

LEUSCHEL, MAX. *Autobiographisches in Smollett's "Roderick Random."* Leipzig, 1903.

LIND, RICHARD. *An Essay on the most Effectual Means of Preserving the Health of Seamen*. London, 1757.

London Magazine, The. I–LIV (1732–1785).

McKILLOP, ALAN D. "Notes on Smollett," in *PQ*, VII (Oct., 1928), 368–374.

MACMILLAN, DOUGALD. *Drury Lane Calendar (1747–1776)*. Oxford, 1938.

MANWARING, G. E. *A Bibliography of British Naval History*. London, 1930.

MARRYATT, FREDERICK. *Snarleyow*. London, 1897.

MASEFIELD, JOHN. Introduction to Richard Hakluyt, *Principal Navigations*. New York [n.d.]. Introduction to Richard Walter, *A Voyage Round the World ... by George Anson*. New York, 1930. *Sea Life in Nelson's Time*. New York, 1925.

MOLYNEUX, THOMAS. *Conjunct Expeditions ... Carried on by the Fleet and Army*. London, 1759.

[MONCRIEF, JOHN.] *Galba: a Dialogue on the Navy*. London, 1748.

Monthly Review, The. I–LXXIII (1748–1785).

MOORE, F. FRANKFORT. *The Life of Oliver Goldsmith*. New York, 1911.

MOORE, JOHN. Life of Smollett prefixed to *The Works of Tobias Smollett*. I (London, 1797).

MORRIS, JOHN. "Was Goldsmith a physician?" in *Journal of Amer. Med. Assoc.*, XXVI (May 16, 1898), 953–957.

MYERS, I. A. "Tobias Smollett," in *Hygeia*, VII (May, 1929), 504–507.

NAMIER, LEWIS. *The Structure of Politics at the Accession of George III*. 2 vols. London, 1929.

NANGLE, BENJAMIN CHRISTIE. *The Monthly Review, First Series, 1749–1789, Indexes of Contributors and Articles*. Oxford, 1934.

NATHAN, GEORGE JEAN. "Bookworms of the Sea," in *Bookman*, XXIX (July, 1909), 483–485.

NICHOLS, JOHN. *Illustrations of the Literary History of the Eighteenth Century*. 8 vols. London, 1817–1858. *Literary Anecdotes of the Eighteenth Century*. 9 vols. London, 1812–1816.

NICOLL, ALLARDYCE. *A History of the Late Eighteenth Century Drama 1750–1800*. Cambridge [Eng.], 1927.

NIXON, J. "Further notes on Thomas Dover," in *Proceedings of the Royal Society of Medicine*, VI (May 29, 1913), 233–237.

NOBBE, GEORGE. *The North Briton*. New York, 1939. (Columbia Univ. Studies in ... Literature. No. 140.)

NORDHOFF, CHARLES, and HALL, JAMES. *Mutiny on the Bounty*. New York, 1932.

NORTHCOTE, WILLIAM. *The Marine Practice of Physic and Surgery*. 2 vols. London, 1770.

NOYES, EDWARD S. "Another Smollett letter," in *MLN*, XLII (April, 1927), 231–235.

OEXMELIN, ALEXANDER. *Histoire des Avanturiers*. 2 vols. Paris, 1688.

OSLER, WILLIAM. "Thomas Dover, M.D.," in *Johns Hopkins Hospital Bulletin*, VII (1896), 1–6.

PAGE, EUGENE R. *George Colman the Elder*. New York, 1935.

PARKER, ADMIRAL SIR HYDE. "Order Book ... whilst Commander-in-Chief at Jamaica, August 13, 1799, to July 15, 1800." MS at New York Public Library.

PARRY, ELSIE. "When literature went to sea," in *Bookman*, LXXV (June and July, 1932), 243–248.

PEPYS, SAMUEL, *Diary*. Ed. H. Wheatley. London, 1924.

P[ERRIN]., W. G. "Tobias George Smollett," in *The Mariner's Mirror*, X (Jan., 1924), 94.

PLOMMER, H. R. [and others]. *A Dictionary of Printers and Booksellers in England, Scotland, and Ireland, 1726–1775*. [London] 1932.

POTTLE, F. A. "A North Briton extraordinary," in *NQ*, CXLVII (Oct. 11, and Dec. 6, 1924), 259–260.

POWELL, L. F. "William Huggins and Tobias Smollett," in *MP*, XXXIV (Nov., 1936), 179–192.

PRINGLE, JOHN. "A discourse upon some late improvements for preserving the health of mariners," in James Cook, *A Voyage towards the South Pole, and Round the World*, II (London, 1777), pp. 369–396.

RICHMOND, HERBERT. *The Navy in the War of 1739–1748*. 3 vols. Cambridge [Eng.], 1920.

ROBBERDS, HENRY. *William Taylor of Norwich.* 2 vols. London, 1843.

ROBINSON, CHARLES, and LEYLAND, JOHN. *The British Tar in Fact and Fiction.* London, 1909.

ROSS, ERNEST. "The Development of the English Sea Novel." Dissertation, the University of Virginia, 1927.

[SARGENT, W.] "Some inedited memorials of Smollett," in *Atlantic Monthly,* III (June, 1859), 693–703.

S[CHUYLER]., E. "Tobias Smollett in search of health," in *Nation,* XLVIII (May 23 and 30, 1889), 423–425, 444–445.

Scots Magazine, The. I–XXXIII (1738–1771).

SCOTT, TEMPLE. *Oliver Goldsmith.* New York, 1928.

SCOTT, WALTER. Memoir prefixed to *The Select Works of Tobias Smollett,* I (Philadelphia, 1833), pp. 11–25.

SECCOMBE, THOMAS. "Smollett, Tobias George," in *BNB.* "Smollett, Tobias George," in *Ency. Brit.,* 11th ed.

SHADWELL, CHARLES. *The Fair Quaker of Deal: or, The Humours of the Navy.* London, 1737. Same. Altered by Edward Thompson. 2d ed. London, 1775.

SHARP, SAMUEL. *A Critical Enquiry into the Present State of Surgery.* London, 1754.

SMEATON, OLIPHANT. *Tobias Smollett.* New York [1897].

SMELLIE, WILLIAM. *A Treatise on Midwifery.* 3 vols. London, 1876–1878.

SMITH, JOHN. *The Travels and Works.* 2 vols. Edinburgh, 1910.

SMOLLETT, TOBIAS. *A Complete History of England.* 4 vols. London, 1757–1758. *The History of England from the Revolution to the Death of George II.* 5 vols. London, 1807. [First pub. 1789.] *An Essay on the External Use of Water.* Ed. Claude E. Jones. Baltimore, 1935. [First pub. 1752.] *The Letters.* Ed. Edward S. Noyes. Cambridge [Mass.], 1926. "Observation on the separation of the pubic joint during pregnancy," in Smellie, *op. cit.,* II, pp. 8–9. [attrib. au.] *A Sorrowful Ditty.* London, 1752. *Travels through France and Italy.* Ed. Thomas Seccombe. London [1919. First pub. 1766]. "The unfortunate lovers," in *British Magazine,* I (May, 1760), 121–125. *The Works.* Ed. W. E. Henley [and others]. 12 vols. Westminster and New York, 1899–1901. [First publications: *Roderick Random,* 1748; *Regicide,* 1748; *Peregrine Pickle,* 1751; *Fathom,* 1753; *Compendium of Voyages* (including Smollett's *Account*), 1756; *Reprisal,* 1757; *Greaves,* 1762; *Atom,* 1768; *Humphrey Clinker,* 1771.]

STOCKDALE, PERCIVAL. *The Memoirs of Percival Stockdale,* written by himself. 2 vols. London, 1809.

[THOMPSON, EDWARD.] *The Courtesan.* London, 1765. Seaman's Letters. London, 1756.

TURBERVILLE, A. S. (ed.). *Johnson's England.* 2 vols. Oxford, 1933.

Universal Magazine, The. I–LXXVI (1747–1785).

Universal Visiter, The. I (1756). All published.

[VERNON, EDWARD.] *Adm. V . . . n's Opinion upon the Present State of the Navy.* London, 1744. *A Letter to the Secretary.* London, 1744. *Original Papers Relating to the Expedition to Carthagena.* London, 1740. *Some Seasonable Advice.* London, 1746.

WALTER, RICHARD. *A Voyage Round the World . . . by George Anson.* New York, 1930.

WARD, JOHN. *The Wooden World Dissected.* London, 1929.

[WATKINS, FREDERICK.] *The Young Naval Hero.* London, 1807.

WATSON, HAROLD F. *The Sailor in English Fiction and Drama, 1550–1800.* New York, 1831.

WHITRIDGE, ARNOLD. *Tobias Smollett.* [New York], 1925.

WILLIAMS, IOLO A. *Seven XVIIIth Century Bibliographies.* London, 1924.